BEHAVIOR, DEVELOPMENT, AND TRAINING OF THE HORSE

BEHAVIOR, DEVELOPMENT, AND TRAINING OF THE HORSE

FREDERIC J. SAUTTER

JOHN A. GLOVER

ARCO PUBLISHING, INC.
NEW YORK

Published by Arco Publishing, Inc.
219 Park Avenue South, New York, N.Y. 10003

Library of Congress Cataloging in Publication Data

Sautter, Frederic J
   Behavior, development, and training of the horse.

   Bibliography: p. 139
   Includes index.
   1. Horse—Behavior. 2. Horses—Psychology.
3. Horse-training. I. Glover, John A., 1949–
joint author. II. Title.

SF281.S28   636.1′083′019   80-23654

ISBN 0-668-04809-3

Printed in the United States of America

Contents

BEHAVIOR, DEVELOPMENT, AND TRAINING OF THE HORSE

CHAPTER 1

An Introduction to Equine Psychology

The horse has a long and illustrious history of companionship with human beings. In the five or six thousand years since it was domesticated, the horse has had a greater impact on human life than any other animal. Other animals may have been domesticated before the horse—say cattle, sheep, pigs, or dogs—but none ever achieved the very special comrade-in-arms relationship of horses and humans.

If the horse had never been domesticated, the history of the world would be so very different that we cannot even guess the changes. Without the horse, the American West would not have been effectively settled. Genghis Khan and his Mongol hordes could not have overrun much of the world. The Roman Empire would not have been overthrown by barbarians. Conquerors in chariots would not have swept over Europe and the Mideast in 2000 B.C. The history of mankind, at least until the early 1900s, is also the history of the horse and no such claim can be made for any other animal.

Evidence gathered from excavations of prehistoric villages demonstrates that the horse was once a game animal. Later, the horse was raised as a source of meat and milk. From time to time, it was even worshipped, but the most important function of the horse has been, of course, its role as a beast of burden. Carrying people and packs, pulling wagons and plows more effectively than any means (other than the recently developed internal combustion engine)—the horse made history.

In the last sixty years, the role of the horse in our society has changed drastically. As we drive our cars down the highways we pass fields where huge tractors and combines do the work that horses once did. Tractor-trailer trucks whiz by us, carrying loads that were once carried by horses. In fact, as we pass other cars, we can reflect on the fact that our internal combustion carriages have also replaced the horse.

Because of technological advances the horse is no longer a necessity here in the United States. Oh, a few poor farmers still use mules for farming and there are some diehards who use horses or burros as pack animals, but any real *need* for the horse has almost completely disappeared. It's no longer the mainstay of American agriculture, commerce or travel, and not unexpectedly the horse population has dwindled from its peak of 20 million in 1920 to fewer than four million today. But that so many horses are maintained by so many people, often at great expense and inconvenience, shows that something about the horse continues to make it appealing.

To own a horse or even to want to own a horse is illogical. Horses require care, affection, special feeding, veterinary care and an area in which to romp and exercise. A useful horse must be carefully trained. Owning a horse is expensive, costing both money and time. A stall and pasture lands must be owned or rented, and food must be grown or purchased. Water must be available. Even with the cost of gas, owning a car is cheaper for most of us than owning a horse. Your car doesn't need affection. Your car doesn't need training or exercise. Plus, a car will get you where you want to go faster, easier, more safely and more cheaply than a horse will. There *is* that certain something about horses, though.

People rarely own horses for utilitarian purposes any more. No doubt the utility of the horse played a very important part in the original domestication of the horse, but it doesn't matter much now. No, it seems that today people own horses because of the horse's basic nature—its intelligence, its courage and especially its affectionate nature.

A horse's affection must be earned. Once this affection has been earned, it is a highly rewarding and valuable commodity. Among horse owners, the knowledge that they are being granted affection by an independent being, that they have earned this reward, is what makes them enthusiastic horse lovers.

WHY THE HORSE?

To understand why the horse is so important to so many people we must look at not only the needs of the people (for travel, companionship, affection, etc.) but the behavioral characteristics of the horse as well.

One of the first reasons that people choose horses over (or in addition to) other pets is because of the native intelligence of the animal. Intelligence is a criterion upon which we would dismiss thousands of animals as possible pets. We might keep a lizard or a turtle as an oddity, and we might cage scorpions to impress our friends, but we could not possibly recommend such animals as pets. They could not even learn the simplest behaviors. Imagine trying to teach a tarantula to come to you. In fact, without intelligence many animals would be dangerous to us. It's unlikely that we would be able to inhibit their natural tendencies to bite, strike out, kick, constrict—whatever the case may be. Without that special spark of intelligence that we see in certain animals, it is unlikely that we could ever form a friendship bond with them. Anyone who has ever watched a well-trained horse go through its paces or watched a horse figure out how to open a latch can attest to the fact that horses are intelligent just as anyone who's shared much time with a horse can attest to its affection.

Intelligence by itself, though, is not enough to account for why so many people go to such great expense to keep horses. If we were to study all the animal species on the face of the Earth (and in the oceans) we would find a great number as intelligent or more intelligent than the horse. Chimpanzees, gorillas, lemurs, porpoises and killer whales are some species that are probably more intelligent than the horse. These animals are capable of learning the same kinds of tasks we teach the horse (given that they have the physical structure to do them) and many tasks more complex than can be learned by the horse. Nonhuman primates are capable of learning hundreds of words in sign language. Intelligence, no matter how important, cannot by itself account for the tremendous popularity of the horse. To try and account for the popularity of the horse we must look for some other reason. That reason can be stated in one word: personality. The personality of the horse is a personality that is suitable for domestication.

If we examine the interaction between horses and humans, it is easy to see how the personality of the horse fits into the broader pattern of human behaviors. The horse possesses traits that complement the traits of human beings.

First, within some rather specific limits, the horse is a social animal. It has lived in groups from two to one hundred. (The population of the true wild horse has been so decimated that we must rely on reports a hundred years old regarding the natural behavior of the species.) Typically one horse is the leader of the herd, with the rest of the herd subservient in varying degrees to it. Common knowledge inevitably places a stallion at the head of the herd but early reports clearly indicated that females were dominant in herds nearly as often as males. The family unit usually consists of the mare and its foal frequently attached to groups of mares attended by one stallion. A distinct social herd behavior exists among horses, allowing for the smooth functioning of the herd as a social unit.

What does this social behavior in herds have to do with us? Well, the domestic horse treats humans as parts of its herd, easily forming emotional bonds to humans if they are present during specific stages of early development. Some argue that the horse treats humans as though they were the dominant members of a herd; others argue that horses tend to behave towards a human as if the human were part of its own herd. Which theory is true doesn't really matter, for it is the ability of the horse to form emotional and social attachments to humans that is the important point.

How is it that horses form social attachments to humans so easily? The answer lies in the development of the horse. As the horse passes through a critical period of development known as the period of primary socialization, the horse will make permanent social attachments to those individuals who are present. If the foal is surrounded only by the mare and other horses, it will form these attachments solely to horses. If humans are not present during this period, it is extremely difficult to retrain the foal to form social attachments to humans. It's not just a matter of humans and horses: any animal present during the period of primary socialization—dogs, cats, even geese—can have social bonds formed to them by the developing horse, given the proper kinds of interactions.

Working in concert with the development of the horse is a function of developmental psychology. Developmental psychology is that branch of the science of psychology most concerned with human development. Developmental psychologists have solved many of the highly complex problems of learning and development among humans. They have had a tremendous impact on educational practices throughout the United States. It is obvious that some behaviors are most easily learned at some specific developmental stages. As muscles, neural pathways and modes of perception develop, tasks that could not possibly be learned become very easy to learn. Just as a five-year-old can learn to sound out words while a three-year-old cannot, regardless of how much time is spent in teaching, the development of any organism (including horses) is a constant dynamic process where biological growth, maturation and the environment interact to form an adult organism. Thus, a careful examination of the development of the horse, from birth to adulthood, is essential so that we may see what to expect and when to expect it. If we possess a knowledge of the development of the horse we can make better decisions for the teaching of behaviors at those times when the learning will be easiest. We'll also be able to bring about the correct amount of socialization in the animal and avoid problems that have plagued horse owners throughout history.

These problems can be seen in the efforts that have been made to domesticate feral horses, which are wild horses descended from domestic animals. Herds of feral horses are fairly common in North and South America. Some of these herds can have their roots traced back to horses that escaped from the Spaniards in the 1500s. It is extremely difficult if not impossible to truly domesticate an adult feral horse, although its offspring can be easily domesticated if humans are present during the period of primary socialization. If humans are not present during this time, it is necessary to resort to breaking the horses.

Unfortunately, there is very little known about attempts to domesticate Prezewalskii's (Central Asian) horse or the now extinct Tarpon, a wild horse originally from Russia. Diary entries of explorers and naturalists of the 1860s and 1870s, however, confirm the general difficulty in domesticating adult horses.

As we have pointed out, during this period of primary socialization, social attachments can be made to any organisms present. The rapport we see between some horses and Dalmation dogs is a result of such experience. Strong attachments can be formed in as little as seven to ten days during the period of primary socialization even if the contact is only for a brief time each day. Frequent exposure of colts and fillies to humans during this time will ensure sociable horses inclined toward human contact.

The responsibility of owning a horse is a great one. In fact, the term own is not quite correct. We own television sets, pencils and cars. We cannot own an intelligent, living being capable of deciding who should and who should not receive its affection. At any rate, owning a horse requires the provision of proper nutrition, exercise, veterinary care, and training. Improper training has ruined more person-horse relationships than any other factor. Throughout this book we emphasize the responsibilities of the human partner in the horse-human relationship.

THE BENEFITS OF LEARNING A PSYCHOLOGICAL APPROACH TO HORSE BEHAVIOR

The responsible horse owner is a person who is responsive to the horse's needs and is skilled enough to train the horse to be responsive to his or her needs in return. If you are to have a good relationship with your horse, you must have some knowledge of equine psychology. Each person who owns a horse has a unique and individual way of living, which includes specific needs, habits and quirks. We must make the same observation about every horse. Each horse is an absolutely unique organism. Though it has many things in common with other horses, it is still a one-of-a-kind being. To establish a mutually satisfying relationship between horse and human (or horses and humans, as the case may be) a mutual adaptation process that benefits both partners must be developed. Horses are not as adaptive as other creatures and have specific nutritional and exercise needs. However, with proper training techniques a highly satisfactory relationship can be established. Training is necessary—there is no way to avoid it. It can be fairly easy, if the kinds of procedures outlined in this book are followed, or it can be excruciatingly difficult and never actually be successful. The horse must learn our rules but we must also learn some of its rules. Too many owners have suffered the painful or frustrating consequences of poorly trained horses. Poor training is not the horses's fault, it is the owner's. Horses, after all, cannot read training manuals or books about human training. The matter of proper training is our problem but it need not really be a problem. There is no reason to tolerate a poorly trained horse. On the other hand, horses should not have to put up with inappropriate human behavior such as not providing proper exercise, not providing proper nutrition, not providing for proper health care and not providing clean stabling. We quickly find out that horses cannot and will not tolerate such inappropriate behavior on our part. In turn, complex behavior can be taught to horses regardless of how unteachable or untrainable we may have thought them to be. The idea that horses cannot be trained or taught but only broken is false.

Before any kind of training procedure or behavior management procedure can be utilized with horses, the basic psychological concepts from which these techniques are generated must be understood. Any person who has ever worked at training any organism, from a white rat to a horse, can attest to the fact that a knowledge of basic psychological principles is absolutely necessary. Anyone working with animals must understand what variables affect behavior, how they affect behavior and how these variables may be manipulated to change behavior. It is impossible for us to try to describe in any detail how a horse owner may train all the specific behaviors he or she may be interested in; there just isn't enough room in one book. There are so many horse owners, each concerned with the very specific needs of his or her own horse, that we cannot anticipate the needs of all horse owners. Learning the basic psychological principles underlying all behavior management (training) procedures, however, will allow each reader to design his or her own training procedures. Once you understand the factors that affect behavior, the basic techniques of changing behavior and the basic methods for analyzing behavior, you will be able to develop your own unique program for modifying equine behavior.

We have designed and written this book to help you to identify those variables that influence the behavior of your horse. Our approach, in fact, is not limited to equines. After reading this book, you should be able to identify the variables affecting the behavior of any organism. Beyond mere provision of identification, we describe in down-to-earth language how these variables operate. The way in which any organism, from planaria to humans, behaves is the result of a highly complex interaction of a great number of variables. Kuo (1967) categorized the variables that influence behavior into five major groups. Their interaction should be understood in order to understand the behavior of any one animal. These five groups of variables are: (1) the form and structure of the organism; (2) the state of the organism biochemically and biophysically (the biological and chemical factors); (3) those parts of the environment to which the organism reacts; (4) the individual organism's history of physical and emotional development; and (5) the context or frame of reference in which the behavior occurs. When we consider all of these factors together, as we must, we see firstly that the current behavior of your horse is clearly a result of the form and structure of horses. Horses can only do those things allowed by their structure; for example, lateral mobility and walking backwards is extremely difficult for horses and flying (without wings) is impossible. Your horse's biochemical and biophysical state (e.g., fatigue, illness, hunger, thirst, anemia, etc.) is important. Those parts of the environment to which the horse responds play a role. An airplane flying several thousands of feet overhead may be ignored and not affect behavior, while the sweet smell of newly mown hay may have a very powerful effect. The history of your particular horse, including its physical and emotional development, and whatever is happening to the horse at the moment, are all significant.

Examining these five variables with respect to the horse is the purpose of this book. We will, throughout this book, be providing you with information about the form and structure of the horse, the effects of biophysical and biochemical changes on behaviors, the emotional and physical development of the horse, those stimuli in the environment to which horses react most strongly and techniques whereby you may assess the context of equine behavior.

THE COMPARATIVE APPROACH

Whenever we engage in the study of behaviors of organisms other than human we are entering that branch of psychology called *comparative psychology*. The study of human behavior is not totally rejected, but it is only on the fringes of comparative psychology. A horse owner who has taken the care and time to learn about the intricacies of horse behavior can take pride in referring to him/herself as a comparative psychologist.

We have had many people ask us why there should be such a discipline as comparative psychology. Why indeed should a distinct branch of psychology be devoted to the study of nonhuman behavior? Ratner and Denny (1964) provide four reasons for the existence of comparative psychology. Since you the reader are about to enter this field (although in an admittedly simplified form) it is a good idea to deal with these four reasons here. The first and most obvious reason for studying an animal is to gain more knowledge about that particular animal. Zoologists, for example, study the various animal species because they believe that all species are inherently interesting and potentially valuable and useful. Crossbreeds such as the beefalo, a cross between American Bison and Cattle, have resulted directly from studies of both cattle and bison. While still relatively scarce, the beefalo may be *the* meat animal of the future. It seems to possess the best characteristics of both the bison and the cow.

Another reason for studying animal behavior is of great importance to all of us. Each year consumers save millions of dollars as the result of advancements in animal science gained through studying particularly the domestic animals, horses, cattle, sheep, goats, etc. Not only is careful attention given to the nurturance of those animals believed valuable, but many studies are conducted to help reduce problems from those animals perceived as pests. Thorough knowledge of the behavior predators—the coyote for example—allows animal breeders to control these predators and save themselves and ultimately the consumer thousands of dollars without endangering the animals.

The use of an animal as a model system is the third reason for comparative psychology. There are a great many conditions in human life that we would like to rectify. However, we cannot ethically or morally study the effect of, say, the consumption of lead on brain damage in humans. If we want to know what the effects of various chemicals are on the human body (including cyclamates, saccharine and food dyes), if we want to induce ulcers or cause heart diseases so that we may gain knowledge to combat these illnesses or if we want to know if new miracle drugs work, we cannot reasonably study human beings. Our only choice is the use of lower organisms as models for what might happen to humans. Animals are important as models of human systems for studying all those problems to which we dare not expose ourselves. We are aware that many people believe that this sort of research is inhumane. Even so, this sort of research must be conducted to reduce human suffering. If 10,000 white rats die so that one human baby lives, we feel this a good tradeoff, indeed. We feel, in fact, that no number of white rats could have the value of one human life. Very stringent guidelines are imposed on all animal laboratories by state and federal agencies which limit to the greatest extent possible unnecessary mistreatment of animals. Many dogs and cats have died, in a very literal sense, for their masters.

The fourth reason for the study of comparative psychology is to develop systems of analyses of similar behaviors across many kinds of animal life. The comparative analysis approach is a complex one that attempts to produce general psychological theories demonstrating the relationship of similar kinds of experiments conducted with many different species of animals. One example of this kind of research may be seen in those studies which investigate the effect of mother presence or absence in many species during early development. Some studies were done with monkeys and later, with other species. After a careful analysis of an extensive amount or research data, the results were related to what was known about humans who had been in situations where they had been deprived of sufficient maternal contact. The results, taken together, gave us a clearer picture of the importance of maternal contact. As a result of research conducted over a wide variety of species, we have a much better understanding of the effects of deprivation of maternal contact.

Data Gathering in Comparative Psychology

Now that you can see what comparative psychology is and why this field exists, we can examine how data (evidence, results, knowledge) are gathered by comparative psychology through the field (naturalistic) method and the experimental (laboratory) method.

The field method is most frequently used by a group of scientists known as ethologists. Ethology is that discipline devoted to the study of the behavior of organisms in their natural environment. Ethologists have been primarily engaged in classifying behaviors, studying instincts and studying and refining the structure of evolution theory (Ratner and Denny, 1964). The most important contribution to the knowledge of behavior by ethologists is generally considered to be the data they have gathered in the areas of innate behavior and social behavior of organisms in their natural habitats. Outstanding ethologists (Tinbergen, 1951; Lorenz, 1957) have introduced concepts into the study of behavior that have become important to all students of behavior.

One of the ethological precepts that has gained widespread currency in all studies of behavior is the concept of *fixed action patterns*. Fixed action patterns refer to a series of behaviors that are usually performed by an animal in the presence of certain specific stimuli. To an observer, the animal seems to perceive a specific stimulus. As soon as it perceives the stimulus, the organism emits a response, seemingly without any possible time for mediation (thinking) between the perception of the stimulus and the appearance of the response. The organism seems machine-like; perception immediately followed by response. A fixed action pattern is a *species specific* phenomenon. That is, it occurs in all members of one species in exactly the same way, but it does not occur in different species. The stimuli that bring forth these fixed action patterns are referred to as *releasers* or *sign stimuli* by ethologists and are also species specific. You should familiarize yourself with these terms, as we shall be using them throughout the remainder of the book. If you are particularly observant, you may already have identified releasers and fixed action patterns which are species specific in horses.

The experimental or laboratory method is used primarily by psychologists. A laboratory approach to studying behavior takes place in a laboratory, as you might well imagine, where the experimenters can precisely and carefully control the conditions in an organism's enviornment. With the use of a good laboratory, we can control almost everything in the environment. Proper equipment allows us to control air pressure; air temperature; humidity; dust in the air; bacteria in the air, food or water; sounds; physical contact; lighting— almost anything you could imagine. We can alter these variables one at a time and determine the influence of each on behavior, or we can vary combinations of them. Such carefully controlled techniques allow us to determine how different parts of the world affect behavior. There is one very real problem with the laboratory method, though. Results that we obtain in a laboratory do not necessarily hold true when generalized into real world situations. The student of behavior, then, must combine information from both experimental and field research in order to obtain the best possible information about the behavior of an organism. The integrated information from both laboratory and field research methods presented in this text will provide you with a holistic and coherent approach to equine behavior.

Theoretical Basis

Since the inception of psychology as a distinct field about one hundred years ago, there have been dozens of different theoretical approaches to the study of behavior espoused by the luminary figures within this field. Some of these theoreti-

cal bases are now no more than historical curiosities for be-
leaguered undergraduate students of psychology to master,
but many of them are still adhered to by large numbers of
practicing psychologists. Since the theoretical orientation of
psychologists is an important point to consider for consumers
of psychological knowledge, we shall take a moment to describe for you our personal orientation. We are both behaviorists, specifically behaviorists of the operant mode. Be-
lieving that operant psychology is the most appropriate basis
for a book of this kind, we have elected to avoid getting
bogged down with hypothetical constructs that emphasize the
internal state of an organism; the complex theoretical constructs used by other theories that cannot be measured or
observed. We also avoid the use of constructs that only suit
theories of human behavior. Our basis shall be the analysis
of observable behavior that can easily be identified by the
reader. You should be able to learn quickly and easily how
to predict and control the behavior of your horse. We also
understand that it is not your goal to learn all about the com-
plexities of experimental psychology and so we shall attempt
to use as little scientific jargon as possible.

The operant approach to behavior analysis involves the
reduction of observable behaviors into their basic parts. The
operant approach is cause-and-effect oriented. We view
stimuli as the causes of behavior (independent variables) and
the response of the horse as the effect (the dependent variables). You will become adept at identifying those stimuli
that control the behavior of your horse. This approach has
been demonstrated to be highly effective in predicting and
controlling the behavior of a great number of species, including cats, dogs, horses and humans.

As you read this book you will be able to see all the influences on the behavior of your horse and you will be able to
control those behaviors in order to develop a highly satisfying horse-human relationship.

WHY THIS BOOK?

This book is written for the horse owner, the horse lover or the person who would like to own a horse. The relationship between human and horse can be highly rewarding for both and this book is designed to help you make your relationships with horses the best possible. We keep horses (or, as some people point out, they allow us to keep them) because the human-horse relationship is a beneficial one. To make such a relationship as fulfilling as possible we need to understand the natural history of the horse. The modern horse—Palomino, Thoroughbred or Clydesdale—is the result of several thousands of years of unique experiences in breeding and selection and to understand the modern horse we must understand the processes and needs that created it.

We must know the answers to questions like: Where and why was the first horse domesticated? What ecological function did the horse perform in human pre-history? Who were the horse's ancestors? Additionally, we have to understand the results of modern (17th to 20th century) selective breeding and how it has affected the horses we keep today. In short, to understand the modern horse, we must try to understand the interaction of the horse and the environment man has created around it over the past thousands of years and then we can go on to understand its behaviors and how to shape them.

CHAPTER 2

The History of the Horse

We suppose that we could sit and try to list all of the functions the horse has performed for humankind over the ages and fill several thousand pages. We are all aware of the obvious uses horses have been put to—hauling, pulling, racing and so forth—but among all the uses of the horse one in particular makes the study of the horse different from the study of any other animal. The horse has served as *the* model of evolution for paleontologists, geneticists and laypeople alike since the 1870s. More complete evidence for evolution is available from fossil remains of horses than for any other known species; so, the horse has been the most studied organism in paleontological circles since O.C. Marsh's citation of fossil remains of the horse as proof of evolution.

In one sense, the vast amount of paleontological information generated about the horse is extremely valuable for our purposes. We can, as you will shortly see, trace the evolution of the horse from its origin to modern times with very little guesswork as to missing links, patterns of evolution or ignorance of those distinctive features that make a horse a horse. In another sense, though, the abundance of information is very confusing. Much of the material (especially prior to 1950) written about the geneology of the horse was designed to make a point, pro or con, in the debate over evolution. It is truly difficult to separate the results of objective scientific inquiry from those derived from materials written to make the facts fit a given theory. Today, we take evolution as a given, regarding it as a natural, dynamic process that is still going on among all organisms (nor do we argue that evolutionary theory is in any way antithetical to religious teachings). So, in our tracing of the history of the horse, keep in mind that we are not presenting an argument for or against evolution. Rather, we are telling the story of an animal whose history you must understand to fully comprehend and appreciate its current status.

There is an additional problem in the study of horse history. So much information has been generated that we must try to sift through it and present you only with those things that are truly valuable to you. Many of the techniques and findings of paleontologists are fascinating and worthy of study in and of themselves, but we can only briefly skim the surface of such matters. If you wish to delve further into the background of this fascinating animal, the bibliography will offer you a good starting point for such a study.

HISTORICAL DATES

Before actually getting into the history of the horse it is necessary to introduce you to some topics that must be understood before our history will make much sense. Geological dating procedures is one of these topics. When we refer to Eohippus existing at one time and Equus existing at another, you should recognize that the dating methods used are somewhat different from what you are accustomed to using.

We can date the time of man's first step on the moon to the year, day, hour, minute and even second. Recent historical occurrences can be dated this way because humans were present and recorded the exact time of the occurrence. As we go back further in time, our dating procedures become less accurate. The date on which the first European entered Dakota territory can only be estimated within a year or two of occurrence. Further back, our dating procedures become even rougher. The construction of the tomb of King Tut can be specified only within decades. During even earlier historical times, we do well to place events within centuries and as we travel further and further back in time our estimates of when things happened become increasingly approximate. Consider the fact that even the date of such a momentous occurrence (for several religions) as the birth of Christ can only be estimated within two or three years of its actual occurrence. It is no wonder then, that when we consider prehuman history our dating procedures, of necessity, become rougher still. Those events that occurred at times before anyone was there to record them cannot be assigned dates in an easy fashion. Given our current level of technology, we can be no more precise about such happenings as the appearance of *Homo sapiens* or the horse than approximate dates designed to allow for hundreds of thousands of years of error. Dating is necessary for us, however, to be able to relate one historical occurrence to another. Geologists have developed a method that allows the dating of occurrences in ways that at least make possible the differentiation of events by rough periods. This method of dating is referred to as geologic time.

Geologic time is based on the formation of different layers of earth. Our discussion of the history of the horse begins with the discovery of fossils at different levels of the Earth's crust, deposited at different times. Fossils are dated according to the time periods ascribed to those formations. The following chart is a brief outline of geologic time divisions.

Era	Period	Epoch	Millions of Years Ago
Cenozoic	Quarternary	Holocene Pleistocene	.5–present 2–.5
	Tertiary	Pliocene Miocene Oligocene Eocene Paleocene	13–2 25–13 36–25 58–36 65–58
Mesozoic	Cretaceous Jurassic Triassic		136–65 190–136 225–190
Paleozoic	Permian Caroniferous Devonian Silurian Ordovician Cambrian		280–225 345–280 405–345 425–405 500–425 600–500
Precambrian			3,980–600

As you can see, geologic time is broken down into four major divisions called eras. Eras are then subdivided into shorter segments of time—periods—which are further subdivided (for the Cenozoic) into still smaller bits of time, epochs. The Precambrian time is not subdivided at all and refers to the very oldest formations on the Earth, those that can be identified only as Precambrian. Precambrian time is not really an era as it is that portion in which we lump together everything that occurred from the Cambrian period back to the actual formation of the Earth itself.

Epochs are listed only for the fairly recent Cenozoic era, representing the increasing accuracy of dating procedures as we come closer and closer to the present time. The dates presented in the right column are approximations. Many geologists prefer to use a chart with periods and epochs that overlap by a few million years to better reflect the coarseness of the time scales.

In tracing our history of the horse, we can skip Precambrian time and, as Scott (1937) points out in his classic work on the history of land mammals, we can also skip over most of the Paleozoic era (there are no known fossil remains of mammals appearing until very late in the era). The late Paleozoic and Mesozoic eras are where we will begin our hunt for the emergence of the horse. For a while, however, we must subsume the history of horses into the general history of mammals.

There are scattered fragments of mammal fossils throughout the Mesozoic era, some dating as far back as the late Permian period. Desmond (1976) presents some convincing arguments to the effect that the evolution of mammals must include the entire Paleozoic era but the evidence is still so fragmentary that we must restrict ourselves to the conditions of the Earth during the Mesozoic era.

The beginning of the Cenozoic era is dramatically marked by the great proliferation of mammals and by the total extinction of dinosaurs, the dominant life form during the Mesozoic era. Something occurred at the end of the Mesozoic era that caused the demise of dinosaurs and allowed mammals to emerge as the dominant life form on Earth.

THE MESOZOIC ERA

Reptiles are and were cold-blooded organisms. They have no internal mechanism to keep their body temperature constant. The fluctuations of the environment and adaptive behaviors (e.g., sunning) govern the body temperature of reptiles. As Desmond (1976) points out, dinosaurs may not have been true reptiles and may have possessed the ability to regulate internal body temperatures to some extent. His arguments are highly logical, based on the most recent findings in paleontology, but even he admits that dinosaurs did not possess the kinds of structures that allowed them to cope with rapidly changing temperatures the way that mammals can. The question of whether dinosaurs actually were or were not warm-blooded is not really important; dinosaurs did become extinct (unless one believes that birds are the direct descendents of dinosaurs, as they well may be) and their extinction seems likely to have been primarily a result of an inability to adapt to changing climactic conditions.

Dinosaurs, the major life forms on Earth for more than one hundred and fifty million years,[1] were adapted for life in areas of the Earth where the climate was relatively warm and, more importantly, stable. Dinosaurs first appeared in the latter part of the Paleozoic era and were dominant by the onset of the Mesozoic. They ranged in size from the huge Brontosaurus, a herbivore, and the fearsome Tyrannosaurus, a carnivore, down to tiny insect-eaters no bigger than chipmunks. Dinosaurs filled every ecological niche in the world now held by mammals. There were grazers, such as the Stegosaurus, carnivores of all sorts, including the Allosaurus, ocean-going dinosaurs of great size and flying dinosaurs, such as the Pterodactyl. Their lives and their dominance of the world depended on two highly critical variables that changed drastically at the end of the Mesozoic era. These two critical variables were the climate of the Earth and the plant life on the Earth.

During the Mesozoic era the climate of the entire Earth was mild. Even the Arctic and Antarctic areas at that time

---

[1] Think about this for a moment. One hundred and fifty million years is an incredible length of time, particularly when you consider that human beings have been dominant for less than five or six thousand years.

possessed vegetation very similar to that found in what is now northern Europe. Of course, there must have been differences between the polar regions and the equatorial regions of the planet, but these differences must have been far less marked than the contrast we view. For similar vegetation to be present throughout the world, there could not be the differences we see today where temperatures range from 120° near the equator to below −100° at the poles. The climate of the Mesozoic era was perfect for animals not capable of regulating internal body temperatures. It was mild and constant, without even the seasonal changes we see today. Oh, seasons were surely possible, after all, the tilt of the Earth's axis as it rotated around the sun insured some seasonal changes.[2] But these changes must have been very mild compared to the +/−125° changes common in the northern hemisphere today.

At the end of the Mesozoic era, something happened to the climate of the Earth to make it much more like the present world and very unlike the world of the Mesozoic era. The seasonal changes in the year became much more severe. We don't think much about it, but in recent years temperatures in Cincinnati, Ohio, for example (one of the authors lives there), and Lincoln, Nebraska, varied from +105° to −25°. This kind of radical change in a short period of time could not have been withstood by dinosaurs. Further, the general climate of the Earth cooled. Polar regions became year-round icecaps. The combination of seasonal changes and the general cooling of the Earth was enough to kill off dinosaurs completely over the next several hundreds of thousands of years. Dinosaurs, whether or not they were truly cold-blooded, could not adapt and so died out. Reptiles in

---

[2] It is within the realm of possibility that the axial tilt of the Earth may have increased since the Mesozoic era but no currently available evidence supports such a hypothesis.

general survived only in small numbers, primarily in equatorial areas, or adapted to semi-hibernetic behavior patterns. The way had been cleared for the emergence of the mammal as the world's dominant form of life.

The changeover at the end of the Mesozoic era was probably a rather slow-moving event as such things go. Certainly if we had been living at the time, we would not have noticed changes in one human lifetime. Some theorists argue that the change in the Earth's climate was abrupt, but more likely hundreds of thousands of years were spanned during the extinction of the dinosaurs. All we know for certain is that the change either occurred faster than dinosaurs could adapt, or they just could not adapt. Reptiles were not totally extinguished. The toads and lizards we see in our yards, the snakes and turtles that inhabit the world today, did adapt to those changes, unlike their relatives, the dinosaurs.

THE WORLD OF MAMMALS

At the beginning of the Cenozoic era, the world was perfectly designed for the proliferation of the mammal. Mammals rapidly (at least in geologic terms) took over all those ecological niches formerly filled by the now-extinct dinosaurs. Mammals specialized into herbivores, insectivores, and carnivores. We are obviously most interested in the herbivores since our modern-day horse is a member of this group. To track down the ancestry of the horse, we will sketch an outline of the animals known as herbivores.

Herbivores are plant eaters, obtaining their primary form of sustenance from the consumption of plants. The group we refer to as herbivores contains many species which are grouped into many orders. Perissodactyla, the group we are interested in, is one of fourteen orders (or seventeen, depending on which group of authorities you choose to consult) of mammals currently in existence, ranging from egg-laying mammals to odd-toed ungulates, including the present-day horse.

There are three suborders of Perissodactyla: Ceratomorpha (the tapirs); Rhinocerotoidea (rhinoceroses); and Hippomorpha (horses, asses and zebras). To continue our history of the horse we must follow the history of Perissodactyla in general and then become more specific as we seek to identify Hippomorpha.

Perissodactyla are related to all other mammals. If the evidence was good enough, we could very likely find one species that was the common ancestor of all current mammals. This common ancestor (the term common ancestor referring to an entire species) arose sometime during the early Triassic period. No better guess can be made as to the time of the emergence of the first warm-blooded, self-regulating animals that could clearly be identified as mammalia.

Over the next several millions of years, this common ancestor radiated across the Earth, replacing reptiles and dinosaurs against whom it could successfully compete, and began to adapt to many different ecological niches. Some of this common ancestor's descendents became carnivores, some became insectovores and others became herbivores or remained omnivores. They adapted their behavior and structure to fit the world as it was where they lived.

As dinosaur carnivores died out, they were replaced by mammal carnivores. As dinosaur herbivores died out, they were replaced by mammal herbivores. By the beginning of the Paleocene epoch, the descendents of this mammalian species had filled the world.

The immediate precursor to the mammal was the therasipid dinosaur who flourished during the early Triassic period. As there were several species of therasipid dinosaurs, it is possible that certain of these could have evolved into mammals. Some authorities argue that as many as nine different species made the transition, others settle on only one. Whichever the case may be, by the early Cretacious, there were five groups of mammals present, Pantotheria, Multituberculata, Symmetrodonta, Tricondonta and Monotremata. Multituberculata was evidently a dead-end form that arose in the Jurassic and died out in the Eocene without leaving any descendents; at least, there is no fossil evidence indicating any transition from Multituberculata to modern mammals. These animals were similar to modern woodchucks.

Symmetrodonta, a rodent-like mammal with symmetrical, three-sided teeth, may or may not have produced offspring that survived until modern times. What we know suggests that this form lasted until the late Cretacious without leaving evidence of transition to later forms. Triconodonta were carnivores that grew to about the size of cats. They too, evidently, were a sterile sidetrack and died out during the late Cretacious.

We still have the Monotremata with us, in forms that may be relatively unchanged from the late Cretacious. The spiny anteater and the duckbill platypus must certainly date back to this time, although specific fossil evidence is available only through the Pleistocene times in Australia (Rower, 1966). It seems very possible that these egg-laying, reptile-like mammals are descended from a separate stock of ancestors. In fact, paleontologists keep these and the fossil remains of extinct, primitive mammals grouped together under the loose heading of primitive mammals.

Pantotheria was the ancestor of all modern mammals, both the marsupials and the more highly developed placental mammals. Eutheria, the first true placental mammal, was able to keep its young inside the body for a considerable length of time, giving birth to rather well-developed offspring. This one fact made the Eutheria more adaptive to the world than egg-layers or marsupials. More and more offspring could survive and mature into adults.

The original Eutheria was probably a small rat-like animal with nocturnal and aboreal (tree dwelling) habits. With the extinction of dinosaurs, this small animal was able to compete so effectively with other mammals that multituberculata, symmetrodonta and triconodonta became extinct, while monotremes and marsupials were almost totally displaced to the southern hemisphere and controlled those areas that were inaccessible to placentals.[3]

Eutheria had six major descendents, the protoinsectovores, insect eaters; cetacea, the whales and dolphins; lagomorpha, rabbits and hares; rodents; carnivores; and protoungulates, the precursors of the horse. Protoungulata appeared on the scene at the very end of the Cretacious period. Protoungulata was the ancestor of all later ungulates, the hoofed animals. One of Protoungulata's descendents was the first Perissodactyla, a member of the horse family. The first true horse was Eohippus, who appeared at the beginning of the Eocene period.

Order Perissodactyla

We will stop tracing the history of the horse for a moment and consider the order to which the horse belongs. The order Perissodactyla is grouped together primarily on the basis of the axis of the foot passing through the middle toe of the foot. There are three suborders of Perissodactyla: Hippomorpha, Ceratomorpha and Rhinocerotoidea. Hippomorpha is

---

[3] Living Marsupials and Monotremes are almost totally restricted to South America and Australia. Evidently, because South America was separated from North America until the last couple of million years, and because Australia has been isolated since the beginning of the Cenozoic era, these organisms survived the onslaught of the placentals. When placentals are introduced to Australia, they quickly take over from the marsupials. The Dingo, for example, has almost totally eliminated the Tasmanian Wolf and the Tasmanian Devil, both Marsupials (Morris, 1965).

represented by one family, Equidae or horses. Ceratomorpha is represented by one family, Tapiridae (the tapirs). Rhinocerotoidea is represented by two subfamilies, one-horned and two-horned rhinoceroses. While these animals seem to be radically different from each other, they all arose from the same basic stock, an animal who was either the little Eohippus or quite similar to it.

Not including the rhinoceros and the tapir, which have survived to our present time, there were many other members of the order Perissodactyla that arose and became extinct during the Cenozoic era. Titantotheres, a huge, hulking grazer with a two-pronged horn flourished through the Oligocene period and at least roughly resembled the rhinoceros. This heavily armored, elephant-sized beast appears to have become extinct because of its poor grazing abilities. Chalicotheres, appearing somewhat more like the horse, developed claws on its front feet, apparently for digging up roots. This beast was truly amazing because it represents the only known animal that developed the jaws of a grazing animal coupled with the development of claws. These beasts survived until the Pleistocene in the warmer regions of Asia and Africa. Chalicotheres was better adapted to the world than Titanotheres but still had not acquired those traits that would allow it to survive until modern times.

There are other extinct relatives of the horse (Simpson, 1951) but none are placed directly in the order Perissodactyla. These beasts may have arisen from the Eohippus but more likely developed from close relatives of Eohippus. A truly fascinating discussion of these beasts may be found in G. G. Simpson's book, *Horses* (1951).

Hippomorpha

As the goal of this book is limited to the history, development and training of the horse, we must now leave our dis-

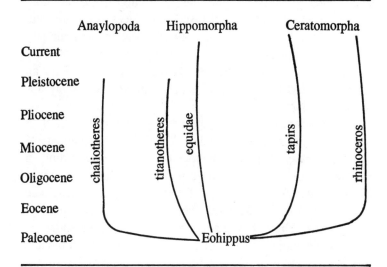

The table above based on Rower's (1966) chart represents the branching of Perissodactyl evolution.

cussion of the relatives of the horse, regardless of how fascinating such a study can be. Hippomorpha is the name for the subgroup of animals that evolved into the horse and although Titanotheres was included in Hippomorpha, we shall not consider that titantic beast any further.

The horse evolved in three very basic ways to give it its current structure: (1) The size of the horse changed from dog-sized (Eohippus) to that of the modern horse; (2) The limb structure of the horse developed into the most highly developed structure among running animals, becoming capable of very rapid forward movement on hard surfaces but almost no ability to complete other forms of movement; and (3) The teeth of the horse developed until they were highly efficient tools for cropping grazing materials, a distinct change from the browsing teeth with which Eohippus started. In general, as the horse evolved it became larger and larger, reaching in its current status the largest size possible for its structure. The legs fused in places and the feet evolved from four functional toes (the thumb was already absent in Eohippus) to one, the center toe being the only functional toe. The teeth developed from forms suited for an omnivorous existence to one suited almost exclusively for plains grazing.

It is important to note that the horse evolved to make it fit into a particular ecological niche. All of the developments of the horse made it more and more capable of succeeding in the function of grazing on large plains. The horse's defense against predators was flat-out forward running speed. The horse's diet was almost exclusively the grass-like vegetation of the plains. The horse, throughout its history, depended on speed as the major ingredient in its survival. The behaviors we see in modern horse, regardless of breed, are a result of the adaptation of Equus to such life. That the modern horse has reached the limit of adaptation to a plains life is fairly evident from the great number of leg injuries to horses during running. The legs cannot adapt further, nor can size increase. Although the horse is no longer subject to natural selection (with the exception of a few wild species) further adaptation would be impossible without radical changes in the basic structure of the horse.

The Descendents of Eohippus

The horse's major line of evolution started with Eohippus, passed through Mesohippus to Parahippus, Merychippus, Pliohippus and ended with Equus. Eohippus was a small, dog-sized beast that was adapted for browsing in forests. Eohippus had four toes on the front feet and three well-developed toes on the back feet. There were definite hooves on this animal. The teeth were suited for browsing rather than grazing. Simpson (1951) has pointed out that Eohippus could have been as fast moving as the whippet. Certainly speed could only have been maintained for short distances. Eohippus seems to have died out by the early Oligocene period.

Mesohippus arose during the beginning of the Oligocene period. This beast was somewhat larger than Eohippus, reaching the size of a large collie. Closely related to Mesohippus was Miohippus, a somewhat larger species. These two species were the first three-toed horses. The middle toe was the largest but all three toes on the front and back feet reached the ground. The teeth of Mesohippus and Miohippus were still best suited for browsing but were gradually adapting for some grazing. These animals were probably still forest dwellers adapted to running on the forest's soft, spongy ground for which their three spreading toes were suited. Mesohippus and Miohippus eventually had at least one set of descendents that became as large as the rhinoceros, Megahippus, but this dead-end species retained the three-toed, forest dwelling configuration of Mesohippus. Mesohippus and Miohippus died out by the end of the Oligocene period but their dead-end ancestors, including Megahippus, may have lasted through the Pliocene.

The third major structural change in the horse is seen in Parahippus. Parahippus first appeared in the Miocene times. Parahippus looked much more like the modern horse because of its elongated skull, a result of the further development of molar teeth. Parahippus still had three toes but the two outer toes were greatly reduced and probably never touched the ground. Parahippus was probably a transitional forest/plains dweller, beginning to develop the traits of the true plains horse. Parahippus was also of a transitional size, probably averaging about the size of a small pony. Merychippus was directly descended from Parahippus. The teeth of Merychippus were similar to the modern horse but this ancestor still had the two outside toes although they were even further reduced than in Parahippus. In size Merychippus was not much larger than Parahippus. Merychippus probably died out at the end of the Miocene although some of its dead-end descendents may have persisted through the beginning of the Pleistocene.

One of the direct descendents of Merychippus was Pliohippus, the direct ancestor of the modern horse. Pliohippus is sometimes found with vestigal outside toes and sometimes not, indicating that it was the true transitional form to one-toed Equus. (Note: Equus does have splints where the two outside toes would be.) Pliohippus thrived during the Pliocene and greatly resembled the modern horse in tooth structure, limb structure and size.

Finally, at the onset of the Pleistocene Epoch Equus itself first appeared. Equus had further reductions of side toes, was somewhat larger and had teeth fully suited to the life of a plains grazer. So, horses as we now recognize them have *only* been in existence for two million years or so. Oddly, horses became extinct in North and South America at the end of the Pleistocene, surviving only in the old world. The plains of North and South America, perfectly suited for horses, did not see any again until they were reintroduced to the western hemisphere by man. Horses arose in North America, spread to every continent except Australia, yet died out in North America. The horse of today, even with all the refinements of selective breeding, is little different than it was two million years ago.

In summary, the horse is a Pleistocene mammal adapted perfectly for life on the plains as a grazer. It evolved from a small forest dweller with browsing habits into its current form through three major changes: limb formation, size and tooth development. Other changes, such as the lengthening of the neck and the shifting of eye further and further back on the skull, followed as a result. Equus is the one surviving family of horse. There were a great number of dead-ends throughout its evolution. The chart pictures the evolution of the horse (see Figure 2–1).

Figure 2–1
Evolution of the Horse

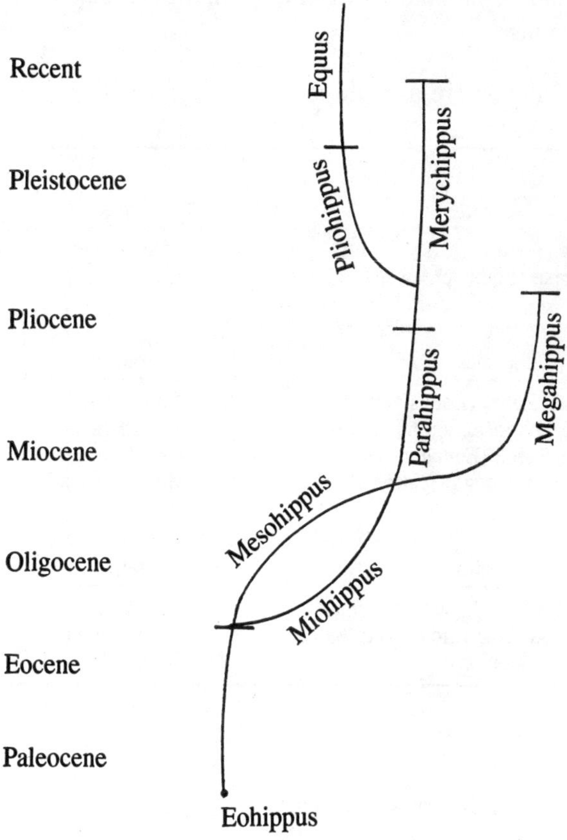

SPECIES OF EQUUS

While it is true that the Equus of today remains relatively unchanged from the beast that emerged at the beginning of the Pleistocene period, there are at least eight contemporary species of Equus (Walker, 1968). Living members of the family of Equus are native to Africa (except the Sahara) and central and eastern Asia. Equus can be grouped into three subgenera, the horses, the zebras and the asses. All these species are relatively similar, differing primarily in size and outward appearance.

The species of Equus are as follows:

HORSES

species	range
Domestic Horse (Equus caballus)	worldwide
Wild Horse (Equus przewalskii)	Central Asia

ZEBRAS

species	range
Mountain Zebra (Equus zebra)	South Africa
Common Zebra (Equus burchelli)	Africa
Grevy's Zebra (Equus grevyi)	Central East Africa
Quagga (Equus quagga) [extinct 1883]	South Africa

ASSES

species	range
Asiatic Wild Ass (Equus hemionus)	Asia
African Wild Ass, domestic (Equus Asinus) donkey	East Africa

NOTE: Mules are the offspring of male asses and female horses. Hinnys are the offspring of male horses and female asses. Zebras have been crossbred with horses but in very limited numbers. Most of the progeny from crossbreeding are sterile. The Tarpon, a wild horse of Russia and Poland, has been extinct for about one hundred years and is not listed here as it may well have been the same species as Przewalskii's horse.

The common names of all these animals are not listed here. There are so many local names and other slang terms used to refer to these animals that a complete listing by origin of use would be impossible. The use of scientific names allows us to avoid the problems of trying to use the correct vernacular names.

Wild Horses

Equus is known throughout the world today primarily as a result of the domestication of *Equus caballus* by humans. True wild horses are only known in the plains of Tibet on both sides of the Altai mountains. The wild horse (*Equus przewalskii*) can interbreed with the domestic horse and the purity of this species is threatened by breeding with the domestic ponies of the region. The wild horse differs from the domestic horse in two ways—it has an erect mane and no forelock. Some of these animals were probably domesticated about 3000 B.C. and formed some of the breeding stock for domestic horses. Wild horses are plains grazers who can go for extended periods (in excess of three days) without water. Their life spans are 25 to 30 years and they escape predators by running. Extinction of this species is likely to come through interbreeding with domestic horses rather than through predation. A closely related species of wild horse, the Tarpon, inhabited the steppes of Eastern Europe and Western Asia until its extinction in the early 1900s. The last Tarpon in captivity died in 1919.

Wild horses, probably numbering fewer than 200, have heavy heads, low-slung tails and a pale red-brown coat that becomes long and shaggy in the winter. The extinct Tarpon was gray and of slighter build. *Equus przewalskii* is of extreme importance to ethologists today as it represents the only true wild horse species in existence. Unless this breed is maintained in captivity it will probably be extinct within the next 50 years.

Domestic Horses Gone Wild

There are such large numbers of wild horses in North and South America that one could easily get the impression that they are native to the areas. During the summer of 1977, in fact, a severe drought in Colorado and Wyoming threatened the lives of so many wild horses that local ranchers shipped in hundreds of tankloads of water to replenish the drinking holes of these animals. There are probably several thousand wild horses in North and South America. These feral horses are the descendents of domestic horses that escaped from captivity during DeSoto's and Coronado's expeditions in the 1500s. Since the plains of North and South America were perfectly suited for horses, they proliferated and, enriched by more escaping horses over the next 400 years, became fully established residents. The specific breeds of horses will be described in another chapter.

Zebras

Zebras inhabit all of Africa except the Sahara and the tropical jungles. They prefer to live in savannahs, plains and occasionally mountain areas. Zebras stand about five feet tall at the shoulder (this is variable within species and across the various species of zebra) and they can reach eight or nine feet in length. The most striking feature of zebras, of course, is their stripes, alternating dark and light bands variously distributed over their bodies.

Equus burchelli, the common zebra, originally ranged from central to southern Africa, although the range has now been reduced. At one time it was thought that there were four distinct species of common zebra but now we know that the variations in coloration that led to the idea that zebras in different areas were different species are a function of where the zebras live. The further north we go in their range, the more distinct the markings; the further south, the less distinct.

The Mountain zebra, *Equus zebra,* is a much smaller, more donkey-like animal than the common zebra. Its range covers the mountainous areas in Africa's cape provinces. Only about 200 of this species still run wild in game preserves. *Equus zebra hartmanne,* a somewhat larger and more numerous relative, lives in wild herds in the mountainous areas of southwest Africa and Angola. All mountain zebras have donkey-like ears, narrow hooves and heavy, donkey-like heads. Evidently the adaptation to mountainous terrain results in these donkey-like traits. In *The Mammals* (1965), Desmond Morris notes that while most zebras are nearly silent, the mountain zebra neighs much like a horse does. The markings on the mountain zebra are variable but tend to gridiron-like patterns on the rump, a unique feature among zebras.

Grevy's zebra, *Equus grevyi,* is the largest of all zebras and has the narrowest stripes. This species of zebra has been known since Roman times. Its range covers Southern Abyssinia, Somalia and East Africa. Grevy's zebra frequently reaches five and one half feet at the shoulder and has a very short (six inch) erect mane. It brays more like a donkey rather than giving the bark of the common zebra or the neigh of the mountain zebra. Additionally, this beast is seen to gallop and trot much like horses and unlike other zebras who usually canter.

The quagga, totally extinct since 1883 when the last specimen died in captivity, has frequently been called half horse-half zebra. The back end of the quagga's body had no stripes at all while the front end was striped only on the head, neck and shoulders. The legs and tail were nearly pure white and the body was a sandy brown color. The quagga inhabited only South Africa where it once was numerous. Its name came from the barking sound it made, "Kwa-ga." The quagga was about four and one half feet high at the shoulder but was very long, reaching nine feet or more.

Asses

Asses are native to Asia, from Mongolia to Syria, and north and eastern Africa. They commonly habitate desert plains that are only sparsely covered with vegetation. Asses are considerably smaller than horses, seldom reaching more than four and one half feet at the shoulder or six and one half feet in length. Characteristic ass features are long ears, small and narrow hooves and heavy heads. Asses also have no forelock and uneven manes. Their eyes are deep-set and their tails are especially long-haired at the tip.

Asses are not characteristically herd animals although groups of up to 100 are occasionally seen in Tibet. These herds break up, though, at foaling time. Asses are particularly well adapted to their dry ranges and are capable of going without water longer than other members of the family of Equus. This ability to work in hot, dry and rough terrain has made them especially suited as pack animals.

There are goodly numbers of wild asses in North America although they, like the horses, are not native. Wild North American asses are the descendents of asses that escaped captivity. It was the African Wild Ass that was the ancestor of the common domestic donkey.

All of the members of the family of Equus have similar habits, fill similar ecological niches wherever they live and are true grazing animals (Cockrum, 1962). All depend on speed for their defense although the ass is much slower than other species. All members of the family can interbreed although many of the crossbred offspring, such as the mule and the hinny, are sterile.

THE HISTORY OF THE DOMESTIC HORSE

The horse is an animal unique in its effect on humanity. No other animal except for the dog (in recent times) has had the kind of relationship with humans that the horse has. Pigs, cattle, dogs, goats and sheep were all domesticated earlier than the horse (Bokonyi, 1974), but the horse changed the patterns of human civilization in more far-reaching ways than any other domestic animal (Clark, 1941).

The horse, with its speed, strength and endurance, greatly altered patterns of travel and communication. It permanently changed the nature of human warfare. The whole pattern of human history was altered by the domestication of the horse. This is clearly seen by the way in which equestrian nomads overran Europe and overcame the Roman Empire, forever changing history.

The horse changed every facet of human life, from transportation to warfare, communication to agriculture, even eating habits. The horse was the first animal to be treated as an individual animal instead of a member of a herd, earning the status of comrade-in-arms with its riders. It was the most important species of domestic animal and, up until the beginning of Christianity, was often buried with its master.

Bokyoni points out that this individual treatment may have doomed the animal. The wild herds were almost wiped out by men who wanted horses. There aren't any left that can survive even on what little space man has afforded them. Then countless generations of breeding have created a very specialized beast. The horse cannot compete with our modern machines. It faces the spectre of being the first domestic animal to become extinct.

The Question of Origin

One of the problems in tracking down the history of the horse is that it was selectively bred so soon after domestication that it's nearly impossible to find a description of the first domestic horse unaltered by selective breeding. And, as there is so much variation in the horse, from the sleek Arabian to the massive Clydesdale, it is particularly difficult to determine if the domestic horse had one or more than one ancestor. Bokonyi (1964) examined the various theories of horse ancestry in great detail. Essentially he recognized six competing theoretical positions.

Samson (1869), one of the first authors to address this problem, postulated a polyphyletic (many ancestor) theory. He believed that there had to have been eight distinct ancestors of the horse. This theory was based on his observation of eight current types (in 1869) of horses. Data gathered since his theory was postulated allows us to dismiss it as an unlikely possibility—we do not recognize eight types of horses.

Skorkowski (1938), using an anthropological technique that differentiated six different skull types of horses, argued that there had to have been a different wild ancestor for each of the skull types he described. Again we can fairly well discount this theory for the reason given above.

Stegmann (1942) classified modern horses into five types and then proceeded to argue that each of these five types had to have had a distinct wild ancestor. Stegmann's position, too, seems untenable given current knowledge.

A classification approach that placed horses into three groups with three wild ancestors was postulated by Ewert (1909) and supported in independent theories by Brinken (1921), Noack (1903), Duerst (1908), Antonius (1922) and Hilzbeimer (1926). This three ancestor theory is very appealing. Although each of the theorists used somewhat different classification approaches, each argues that there are now three distinct types of horse: the warm-blooded horse (e.g., the Arabian), the cold-blooded horse (e.g., the Shropshire) and the ponies. This argument, of course, is supported only if these types are truly distinct and not the result of selective breeding. It appears that the third type, the pony, is not a true distinction. Franck's (1875) examination of the tooth structure of horses seems to indicate that there are only two types, not always clearly distinguishable. More recent evidence (Zeuner, 1963) concerning the ability of the Przewalskii horse and the Tarpon (the only wild species left by the late 1800s) to interbreed with domestic horses and with each other supports the notion that they are of one species.

The majority of practicing horse breeders subscribe to the theory that the horse has dual ancestry. Several researchers in the 1870s and 1880s classified modern horses into two types, the light and the heavy, and argued that there must have been two distinct ancestors. Lundholm (1947) and Ebhardt (1962) agree with this basic position although they differ in defining the types of modern horse.

Finally, there is the monophyletic theory that postulates that all horses are descended from only one common ancestor, a species probably identical to the Przewalskii horse. Herre (1961) and his associates present a great deal of compelling evidence for this theory.

Which theory is correct? We can probably discard all but the last three theories from serious consideration. The ability for eight (or even five) types of horses, descended from different ancestors to interbreed, as they do, stretches the limits of credulity. The strongest evidence would seem to support a monophyletic theory. Today's light (e.g., Arabian) and heavy (e.g., Clydesdale) horses are successfully interbred. If they were domesticated from separate ancestors, those ancestors must have been of the same species with physical differences only as a result of adaption to local environmental needs. The physical differences in these two so-called types of horses do not bear out differences in origin. Differences in their physical structure are superficial, the kinds of differences we see, say, between German shepherds and collies.

Zeuner (1963) in his very careful analysis, concludes that different *ecotypes* of horses were very probably domesticated in separate regions—these ecotypes would be members of the same species who had begun to adapt to different environmental requirements in different areas.

Which of the theories eventually proves correct is of little practical consequence outside of archeology and paleontology. The fact is that all horses can interbreed and that physical differences are, in fact, superficial. Equally interesting questions, ones we are more likely to resolve, are the center of domestication of the horse, the date at which the horse was domesticated and the pattern of domestication.

Centers of Domestication

The pattern of horse domestication is not particularly hard to follow. Evidence from excavations of early human settlements and fragments of early recorded history allow us to feel confident in sketching the process. First, horses were hunted for their meat much as deer were hunted. Then, early in the history of horse-human relations, horses were captured and bred for their meat and milk very much like cattle. The third step was the use of the horse as a beast of burden, eventually resulting in the horse as the puller of chariots and carriages. Finally, the horse was ridden by one person (in the familiar manner). This progression could have gone on in several areas at about the same time but probably did at different rates.

The horse was not, as is popularly assumed, domesticated during the Pleistocene time. The history of domesticated horses begins fairly recently (in historical terms), probably between 3500 and 7000 B.C. An absolute limit of 2000 B.C. is easy to set. The horse-drawn chariot was a common tool of war in 2000 B.C. The horse must have been domesticated prior to this. Bokonyi (1959; 1964; 1974) provides some very convincing evidence for the first center of horse domestication. Historically, he places it at about 3500 B.C. in the settlement of Dereivka. Excavated horse bones at this site leave little doubt that the horse was domesticated here. No determination, of course, could be made as to whether the horse's function was meat animal or beast of burden. This Ukranian village is the earliest known human settlement with horse remains that are definitely domestic. Zeuner's (1963) arguments concerning the availability of wild horses for domestication agrees with Bokonyi's findings. Zeuner concluded, on the basis of the distribution of wild horses, that horses had to have been settled in west and central Europe north of the Alps and eastern Europe and western Asia as far east as Turkistan. Dereivka falls into this area. Western and Central Europe are discounted as centers of domestication because of the scarcity of the horse in those areas' heavy forests.

It is possible that persons in several human settlements in the broad area described by Zeuner domesticated horses independently. After all, humans would be familiar with horses as game and would already have domesticated cattle, sheep, pigs and dogs. Whether or not there was more than one center for domestication really cannot be determined with current evidence. At any rate, the domestication of the horse progressed rapidly. In 1,500 years, horses changed from animals kept for meat to the chariot-pulling comrades-in-arms seen in 2000 B.C. By 2000 B.C., in fact, the horse was known throughout Asia and in much of Europe (Simpson, 1951). The Greeks recorded horses in their history at about 1700 B.C. Egyptians had the horse at about 1600 B.C. The horse was present in India at 1500 B.C. and in Spain by 1200 B.C. Between these times and 1540 A.D. or so, the domesticated horse appeared throughout the known world. As non-horse owners saw people with horses they bartered for them, stole them or domesticated their own.

The horse was reintroduced into the Western hemisphere in the 1540s where it has flourished ever since, in both feral and domesticated forms. The horse is so closely interwoven with American history that no account of it can be written without acknowledging the impact of horses on a great and unsettled continent. The number of horses in the United States kept increasing until about 1920 when there were more than 21 million horses in the United States (Simpson, 1951).

Human society has changed much in the five or six thousand years since the horse was first domesticated, the horse being one of the prime agents of change. The last sixty years, though, have seen a dramatic decline in the number of horses in the world and a change in their function. The horse was finally replaced by the internal combustion engine in the 1920s. Those functions performed by horses before 1920 are now performed by cars, tractors, airplanes and engines of all sorts. In 1960, there were only three million horses in the United States and approximately 61 million worldwide (Sims, 1972).

Today in the United States horses are almost exclusively kept for pleasure. Sims (1972) reports that there are over 3,000 horse shows held annually in the United States, that about 100 polo clubs exist and that there are 100,000 miles of riding trails and over 225,000 horse projects in 4-H Clubs annually. Horse racing, of course, is at its peak in popularity. In one sense the horse has been put out to pasture. Tractors have replaced the horse on farms, trucks have replaced the horse on the highways and cars have replaced the horse in cities and towns. In another sense, though, the horse will likely always be a treasured animal, one that will hold a special place in the hearts of humans as long as there are places to ride horses, people to ride them and, most importantly, people who care.

CHAPTER 3

Breeds of Horses

There are a great many breeds of horses recognized by various organizations as true breeds. Breeds differ from each other primarily in gross size, proportion, coloration and coats. In this chapter we shall briefly identify and describe the major breeds present in the United States, their place of origin, date of introduction to the United States, physical traits and official registration agencies.

Before all this categorization will make much sense you need to know that the height of a horse is measured from the highest part of the withers (the withers are located at the base of the neck, approximating the shoulders) straight to the ground while the horse has its head and neck held in a straight line from its back. The height of horses is expressed in hands and inches, e.g., 15 hands, three inches; usually written 15–3. A hand is equal to four inches.

The age of horses is figured in years as of January first of each year following its birth. For example, a foal born anytime during the calendar year of 1980 would be considered one year old as of January 1, 1981. Hence, it is possible for an 11½-month-old horse and a 10-day-old horse to be classed as the same age. South of the equator, the age of horses is figured from August fourth of each year in the same way.

For our purposes, we will break horse breeds into light horses, draught horses and ponies. The distinction between light horses and ponies is an artificial one which depends on a person's point of view. However, as these distinctions are frequently used we will retain them.

LIGHT HORSES

Arabian

The oldest known breed of horse is the Arabian, which has a documented history reaching back to at least 700 A.D. The Arabian has been the light horse most influential in horse breeding. All other light horses, at one time or another, were developed in part with the addition of Arabian blood lines. The Arabian is the prototypical light horse.

The Arabian horse was developed in Arabia and perhaps southwestern Asia as well. It was first introduced to the United States in 1765 although there is good reason to believe that the horses introduced to the new worlds by Spanish conquistadors had much Arabian blood. (Saying that a horse has certain blood in it or that it is of a particular bloodline, is, of course, a euphemism for referring to parentage. Hence, a horse with Arabian blood is a horse that had an Arabian ancestor. These terms are left over from the days prior to the theories of genetics.)

The Arabian horse ranges from 14–3 to 15–0 hands in height and commonly weighs between 840 and 1,000 pounds. While broken or spotted colors are not good in terms of official registration and show, many Arabians have mottled coats. The preferred Arabian has a solid color with or without white markings. The face of the Arabian is very angular, appearing to be chiseled; its neck is very well arched and its back is short.

The major use of the Arabian, as with nearly all horses nowadays, is for pleasure riding. The Arabian is shown with either English or Western equipment. Registered Arabians in this country can have their history traced back to an Arabian named Ranger who was introduced in Connecticut in 1765. Bay (dull red to yellow-brown) is the most prized color.

Thoroughbred

The Thoroughbred was developed in England and records of Thoroughbred races date back as far as 1377. All Thoroughbreds trace their ancestry to three Arabian sires. It is likely that they were originally bred to Arabian mares and that considerable Arabian blood was bred into the line at first. Now Thoroughbreds are exclusively bred with one another. The word Thoroughbred comes from the literal translation of the Arabian word *kehilan*.

The Thoroughbred was first introduced into the United States in 1730 and has contributed to the breeding stock of many horses developed here. The major use of the Thoroughbred is racing. The Thoroughbred ranges from 15–0 to 16–2 hands and weighs approximately 1,000 pounds. They are not judged by color. Speed is the most important variable in judging the worth of a Thoroughbred. Most Thoroughbreds in the United States are bays.

American Saddle Horse

The American Saddle horse was developed in the southwestern part of the United States not long after 1800. The breeding stock included Thoroughbreds, Arabians, Morgans, Canadian Pacers and Standardbreds. (Note: Some of the breeding stock was introduced long after the American Saddle Horse originated.) This attractive horse is used for pleasure riding and is shown with English riding equipment. Show class American Saddle horses should be of dark solid colors with white markings. The most desirable colors are chestnut (yellow hairs in different shades from golden to liver–the mane and tail are usually lighter or darker than the body color), bay, brown and black. The American Saddle horse varies from 15–0 to 16–2 hands and weighs between 1,000 and 1,200 pounds. Show horses frequently have their tails set. This practice amounts to breaking the tail and then setting it (much as a bone is set in a splint) so that it grows back with the tail up nearly vertically and the hairs then billowing down. Some authorities refer to this procedure as cruel, as it can be painful and limits the horse's use of the tail for swatting flies and so forth. No doubt the owners of set horses disagree.

Morgan

The Morgan horse was developed in Vermont in 1789 of an uncertain ancestry, although Arabian and Thoroughbred ancestry must have been dominant. The Morgan is particularly suited to trail riding although it is an all-purpose pleasure horse. Morgans can be of all normal horse colors but dark colors are the most prized. The Morgan is particularly well known for its intelligence and even temperament. It's one of the least nervous of all horses.The Morgan ranges from 14–2 to 15–2 hands and weighs from 1,000 to about 1,200 pounds.

Standardbred

The Standardbred, sometimes called the American Trotter, was developed in the 1880s as a utility buggy horse. First bred in the eastern United States, the Standardbred has Thoroughbred, Morgan, Arabian, Barb, Norfolk Trotter and Canadian Trotter ancestry. Bay is the most common color but speed in trotting or pacing is the Standardbred's most important criterion. The Standardbred ranges from 14–2 to

16–2 hands and weighs between 800 and 1,300 pounds. They are pleasure horses but are most renowned as harness racers.

American Albino

The American Albino is a recent breed development, bred at C.R. and H.B. Thompson's White Horse Ranch in Naper, Nebraska, in 1918. The Albino was developed by breeding Morgan mares to an all-white stallion, Old King. The American Albino is not a true albino because pigmentation is present, usually in the eyes and extremities. The coat is all white and the skin is pink. American Albinos are mostly used as trick horses or for exhibition purposes. Their height varies from 14–0 to 16–0 hands and their weight ranges from 1,000 to about 1,200 pounds.

Appaloosa

The Appaloosa was developed by Nez Perce Indians in the Paloosa River region of Washington and Oregon. It is thought to have originated around 1730 and was the descendent of Spanish horses first introduced to Mexico. The Appaloosa must be at least 14 hands tall for registration purposes but can be shorter than this and can range up to 15–3. Weight ranges from 900 to about 1,200 pounds. The Appaloosa is a western utility and stock horse although it is now ridden primarily for pleasure.

The Appaloosa's spotted color pattern is its unique characteristic. The eyes have whites much like human eyes. The hooves are black with white vertical stripes. All the basic horse colors may be seen in the Appaloosa but the spotting is always white. The back behind the midpoint (the loin) and the upper parts of the back legs are primarily white with small patches of the dominant coat color.

The Appaloosa is the lone American representative of a very well known phenotype of horse. Spotted horses have been known throughout history. Some arose in Arabia and spread to India, where spotted horses still exist. Summerhays (1966) mentions that Chinese paintings of 3,000 years ago represent horses with markings which are similar to the Appaloosa.

The Pinto and the Paint

Depending on the authority you consult, Pintos and Paints may be considered as one breed or two. They may be registered jointly as both Pintos and Paints, although separate registry is also common. We shall describe them together and note the distinctions. The Pinto and the Paint originated in the southwestern United States. They were originally bred by Indians from those horses introduced to Mexico by Spaniards. The Pinto, generally a smaller horse than the Paint, ranges from 12 to 16 hands. The Paint ranges from 14 hands up. The Pinto weighs from 750 to 1,100 pounds while the Paint usually ranges from 900 to 1,100 pounds. For show purposes, pacers are generally excluded from Paint categories although they are permissible in Pinto categories. Both the Pinto and the Paint have splashes of dark or light that contrast with the basic body color. Two patterns are recognized. The Tobiano pattern consists of dark splashes on a white body while the Overo pattern consists of white splotches on a dark body color. These two patterns are very similar to the *piebald* pattern, large and irregular patches of black and white, or the *skewbald* pattern, large irregular white patches on a background of any other dark color except black. The demarcation between the different colors is usually very clearly defined.

Both the Paint and the Pinto are now primarily pleasure horses although they once were highly prized by cowboys and Indians as excellent working horses. For show purposes the coloration and definition of color is more important than breeding background.

The Palomino

The Palomino is a color type of horse and not a true breed. Color is all important in determining the value of a Palomino. The typical colors of a Palomino are a gold to golden-chestnut body with flaxen to chalk-white manes and tails. White markings are frowned upon in the United States although they are considered permissible in Great Britain, as long as they are not extensive enough to give the appearance of skewbald coloring.

The Palomino is probably of Arabian origin and may date back to Homeric times. The Palomino was highly prized in Spain. Queen Isabella (who sponsored Christopher Columbus) gave such encouragement to the breeding of these horses that they were called "Y'abelles." The name Palomino probably comes from Juan de Palomino, who obtained some of these horses from Cortez.

American breeders became extremely interested in the Palomino around 1900 and developed the American Palomino by breeding for color from among Arabian, Standardbred, Thoroughbred, Tennessee Walking and Quarter horses. They range from 14–2 to 16–0 hands in height and weigh between 900 and 1,200 pounds. They are used entirely for pleasure and are extremely popular show horses.

Barb

The Barb is an ancient breed which originated in Algeria and Morocco. It stood between 14–0 and 15–3 hands and very closely resembled the Arab. The manes and tails were particularly bushy and the tail was lower than the Arabian. Additionally, the shoulders were flatter, the chest more rounded and the head longer than the Arab. The Barb may not exist in purebred form any more but it was one of the basic breeding stocks from which modern horses were developed. No official registration agencies exist in the United States for Barbs. We can estimate that Barbs were probably introduced in the United States before 1800.

Quarter Horses

The Quarter horse has been recognized for two outstanding features, speed in the quarter mile and the ability to work livestock. The Quarter horse originated in the southwestern United States during the last half of the 19th century and was developed from Barb, Arab and Turk types introduced to that region by Spaniards. The first registered Quarter horses came from crosses of the original Quarter horse with Thoroughbreds, Arabs, Standardbreds and Morgans.

English authorities tend to differ with American authorities on the origin of the Quarter horse. Summerhays (1966), for example, maintains that Quarter horses were the descendants of Thoroughbreds, particularly a stallion named Magus, and were used for racing on quarter-mile tracks. The American Quarter Horse Association, however, adheres to the southwestern United States origin as the correct theory.

The Quarter horse stands between 14–2 and 15–2 hands and varies from 950 to 1,200 pounds. Today it is primarily a pleasure horse but is still extensively used in the American West as a livestock worker. All normal horse colors can fit into the Quarter horse type except for Pinto, Paint, Appaloosa or Albino configurations. Darker colors are typically preferred.

Tennessee Walking Horse

The Tennessee Walking Horse is one of the most beautiful animals ever to walk the face of the Earth. It was developed in and around Tennessee from a mixed ancestry but with Canadian Pacer blood clearly evident. The breed was developed about 1890 and was originally known as the Plantation Walking Horse. No one who has ever seen a Tennessee Walker go through its paces could ever forget the beautiful high-stepping walk which is its major characteristic. All normal horse colors may be represented in Tennessee Walking Horses although black, chestnut and roan (a mix of white hair in the coat which makes black appear blueish, bays appear reddish and chestnuts appear somewhat pinkish) are most common. White markings are frequently seen on the faces and legs of the Tennessee Walking Horse. Its height ranges from 15–0 to 16–2 hands and its weight ranges from 1,000 to 1,200 pounds.

The Hackney

The Hackney is an English horse first introduced to the United States about 1820. The Hackney was bred from Oriental stallions and native mares in the 1700s (Bennett, 1966). The word Hackney actually dates from the Norman invasion of England, Haquenee meaning a general-purpose riding horse. While some American sources indicate that the Hackney and the Norfolk Trotter (now extinct) were one and the same breed, Summerhays described the Norfolk Trotter as one of the ancestors of the Hackney and not the same breed at all. In any event, there is a good deal of confusion about this carriage horse because of the use of the word hackney to stand for any horse. The Hackney Horse Society was founded in 1884 and the first official registration of this breed did not occur until this date, relatively late in the history of the breed.

The Hackney stands between 15 and 16 hands and weighs between 900 and 1,400 pounds. Hackneys that do not reach 14–2 are classed as ponies even though they are, in fact, foaled by Hackney horses. Bay is the most common color of Hackneys in the United States, but any dark color is acceptable, as are limited white markings.

PONIES

Ponies are horses shorter than 14–2 hands. However any horse used for polo is always a pony regardless of height. (Conversely, an Arab horse is always a horse regardless of height.) There are no important differences between ponies and horses. In fact, the only difference is that of size. Two foals from the same mare by the same stallion could theoretically be placed in different categories. The distinction is entirely an artificial one, as are many of the breed distinctions.

There are several varieties of equines that breed true as ponies. In other words, the variations in size among some breeds is so small that there are no members of these breeds classed as both horses and ponies. In this section we will briefly review some of the better known breeds of ponies.

A Word About British Ponies

There are nine breeds of ponies recognized as native to the British Islands. All nine breeds have been in Britain during recorded history and whether they were brought there from Europe or whether they are truly native cannot be determined. These breeds are the only natural ponies in the world. That is, they are the only breeds that, over many generations, reproduce ponies of the same general size regardless of external conditions. These nine breeds are: (1) Shetland, (2) Connemara, (3) Welsh Mountain Pony, (4) Dartmoor, (5) New Forest, (6) Highland, (7) Exmoor, (8) Fell and (9) Dales. We will discuss the Shetland, Connemara and the Welsh Mountain Pony, and shall describe the other six breeds in brief.

The Shetland

The Shetland Pony is the best known and most beloved of ponies. Its whimsical, friendly appearance has made it the favorite of children for many years. The Shetland originated in the Shetland Islands and in northern Scotland. They were originally used for pulling coal carts up from mines in the north of Scotland. Today it is almost exclusively a pleasure animal cherished by children. The Shetland was introduced to the United States in 1850 and has flourished here ever since. All the common horse colors can be found among Shetlands. In the United States, almost all have a solid coloration, while piebalds and skewbalds are common in Great Britain. A Shetland's height is measured in inches rather than hands and it usually stands between 39 and 44 inches, weighing only 300 to 400 pounds. The Shetland is the smallest of all living ponies but appears to be the strongest member of the equine family in a strength-by-size measure.

The Connemara

The Connemara is an Irish pony, usually 13 to 14 hands in height and weighing between 700 and 850 pounds. The ancestry of the Connemara cannot be determined at this time because of its antiquity, but it has had Arab blood infused in its stock sometime during its history. The Connemara was not introduced to the United States until 1951 and has been used as a pleasure pony, although some are used as jumpers. Most of the common colors of horses, including piebalds and skewbalds, can be found among the Connemara although these are excluded from shows. The original Connemara was predominately gray.

Welsh Mountain Pony

The Welsh Mountain Pony is frequently confused with the Welsh Pony and the Welsh Cob. The Welsh Mountain Pony and the Welsh Cob are seldom seen in the United States. The Welsh Cob is a riding pony particularly prized in Great Britain for its suitability to elderly riders. It is also an excellent trotter and jumper. The Welsh Mountain Pony is one of its ancestors.

The Welsh Pony, of Welsh Mountain Pony, Welsh Cob and Hackney blood, has been well known in the United States since 1884. The maximum height for this pony is 56 inches and its weight seldom exceeds 850 pounds. It is a pleasure pony used for riding, showing or keeping a pet. Most of the normal horse colors are found among Welsh Ponies, although piebald and skewbald are not acceptable for show purposes.

The Welsh Mountain Pony, ancestor of both the Welsh Pony and the Welsh Cob, originated in the highlands of Wales and is so old that its ancestry cannot be determined. This breed is famed for its durability, strength and intelligence. It too may be any of the normal horse colors including piebald and skewbald. Its height is about 12 hands and it commonly weighs less than 750 pounds. Today, it is a pleasure pony most appreciated as a child's mount.

Hackney

The Hackney pony differs from the Hackney horse only in that it is smaller. This reduction in size was achieved by crossbreeding Hackneys with Welsh Ponies. Its height varies from 11–2 to about 14–2 hands while its weight may vary from 700 to 900 pounds. All other characteristics are the same as the Hackney horse.

Pony of the Americas (POA)

The Pony of the Americas was developed in the United States by crossing Appaloosa with Shetland and Welsh Pony stock. The coloration is similar to that of the Appaloosa, and similar guidelines are used for judging these ponies. Their height varies from 45 to 52 inches and their weight is always less than 850 pounds. This pony is an all-purpose riding animal primarily used for pleasure. Its development cannot accurately be pinpointed in time, but a rough estimate of about 1880 is probably close.

Assorted British Ponies

The Dartmoor Pony (12 hands, 600 pounds) is an indigenous pony found in semi-wild states in the Dartmoor district of southwest England. The Dartmoor is an excellent riding pony. Colors are typical horse colors.

The New Forest Pony has been observed since 1000 A.D. as a feral equine in the Hampshire region of southern England. Its height is typically less than 14–2 and averages out to about 13 hands. Arab blood was added to this line in the 1850s. All typical colors can be observed in this breed.

The Highland Pony is the biggest of all the British ponies and is found in the highlands of Scotland and on nearby islands. It ranges between 12–2 and 14–2 hands in height. The Highland Pony Society recognizes three types of this pony, variants in size from very small (on the island of Bara 12–2) to fairly large (on the mainland 14–2). This breed has been frequently crossed with Arabs, so that there is no longer a purity of breed. The Highland Pony can be of any typical horse color.

The Exmoor Pony is found in the Exmoor forest in the southwest of England. It is distinguished by a particularly heavy mane falling to either side of the neck. Most Exmoor ponies are bays, browns or duns. The average height of the Exmoor is about 12–2 hands.

The Fell Pony was once the same breed as the Dale Pony. The Dale has recently been crossed with the Clydesdale, and so that breed now is considerably different. The Fell Pony comes from the western side of the Pennine hills in northern England. Originally the Fell was used to carry lead ores from mines and is a very powerful, durable and sure-footed pony. Its use today is restricted to pleasure. The Fell Pony averages about 13–2 hands and weighs less than 800 pounds. Most Fell Ponies are black or dark brown with bushy manes and tails.

The Dale Pony, as mentioned above, was once the same as the Fell Pony. Crossbreeding with Clydesdales has caused the Dale Pony to lose almost all of its pony characteristics.

DRAUGHT HORSES

Draught horses are typically delineated from light horses by size. Draught horses are heavier, somewhat taller and have much larger barrels (trunks) than light horses. There are five major breeds of draught horses in the United States.

Belgian

The Belgian was introduced to the United States in 1886 from Belgium, naturally, and is the most powerful of the American draught horses. Its height varies from 15–2 to 17–0 hands and its weight ranges from 1,900 pounds to 2,200 pounds. They are usually chestnut, roan or sorrel (yellowish-chestnut) in color. They are commonly used for exhibitions nowadays.

Clydesdale

The Clydesdale is probably the best known draught horse in the United States, frequently seen in exhibitions. The Clydesdale was introduced to Canada in the 1840s and reached the United States soon thereafter. It originated in the Clyde River valley of Scotland and is commonly bay or brown with white facial markings. It varies from 16 to 17 hands high and from 1,700 to 2,000 pounds in weight. The Clydesdale was originated around 1750 by crossing Flemish stallions with local mares.

Shire

The Shire is the largest of all draught horses (16–0 to 17–2 hands; 1,800 to 2,300 pounds). This British horse was introduced to the United States in the 1840s and is said to be able to pull five tons. Bay and brown colors are the most frequent colors of this "Great Horse of England." All Shires have white on their faces, feet and legs. Originally an all-purpose draught horse, the Shire is now used mainly in exhibitions.

Percheron

The Percheron was developed in the La Perche district of France, probably around 1200. It was introduced to the United States in about 1820. Most Percherons are black with white or gray markings on the face, legs and feet. The Percherons vary in height from 16 to 17 hands and weigh from 1,700 to 2,000 pounds.

Suffolk

The Suffolk is the smallest of the American draught horses (15–2 to 16–2 hands; 1,500 to 2,000 pounds). It originated in Suffolk County, England and was introduced to the United States around 1880. Suffolks are almost always a chestnut color. The Suffolk is typically used only for exhibition now, although it once was used extensively as a draught animal.

SUMMARY

The brief listing of breeds we have presented here is fairly representative of those horses found in the United States. Worldwide there are many breeds that we have not mentioned, due to their rarity in the U.S. A complete listing is nearly impossible.

A listing of breed organizations is presented below. Should you wish additional information about any specific breed you may contact the appropriate organization.

Arabian Horse Club Registry of America, Inc.
7801 East Belleview Avenue
Englewood, Colorado 80110

Jockey Club (Thoroughbreds)
300 Park Avenue
New York, New York 10022

American Saddle Horse Breeders Association, Inc.
929 South Fourth Street
Louisville, Kentucky 40203

American Albino Association, Inc.
Crabtree, Oregon 97335

Appaloosa Horse Club
Moscow, Idaho 83843

Morgan Horse Club, Inc.
P.O. Box 2157
Bishop's Corner Branch
West Hartford, Connecticut 06117

American Paint Horse Association
P.O. Box 12487
Fort Worth, Texas 76116

Pinto Horse Association of America, Inc.
P.O. Box 3984
San Diego, California 92103

Palomino Horse Breeders of America
P.O. Box 249
Mineral Wells, Texas 76067

American Quarter Horse Association
P.O. Box 200
Amarillo, Texas 79105

Tennessee Walking Horse Breeders and
Exhibitors Association of America
P.O. Box 87
Lewisburg, Tennessee 37091

United States Trotting Association (Standardbreds)
750 Michigan Avenue
Columbus, Ohio 43205

American Hackney Horse Society (includes ponies)
527 Madison Avenue
New York, New York 10022

American Shetland Pony Club
P.O. Box 2339
West Lafayette, Indiana 47906

American Connemara Pony Society
Rural Route 2
Rochester, Illinois 62563

Pony of the Americas Club, Inc.
P.O. Box 1447
Mason City, Iowa 50401

Welsh Pony Society of America, Inc.
202 North Church Street
West Chester, Pennsylvania 19380

Belgian Draught Horse Corporation of America
Wabash, Indiana 46992

Clydesdale Breeders' Association of the United States
Plymouth, Indiana 46563

American Shire Horse Association
Lynden, Washington 98264

Percheron Horse Association of America
Belmont, Ohio 43718

American Suffolk Horse Association
Lynden, Washington 98264

NOTE: There are a number of other registration organizations but we feel that a complete list of these, many of which are regional, is beyond the scope of this book. Almost all of the associations we listed publish their own journals. Contact the appropriate organization for further information.

CHAPTER 4

Behavioral Genetics and the Horse

This chapter discusses the effects that genetic factors exert upon behavior. The discussion will be a general one and we will not address specific breeding issues. The question that we are primarily concerned with is whether behavior is determined through genetic predisposition or through environmental effects. While there can be no doubt that genetic variables determine much of the physical makeup of an organism, there is considerable debate about the extent to which heredity may influence behavior. The horse owner has undoubtedly heard that some horses are "born nervous" or are "born with spirit and spunk." We think it is highly questionable that any horse is born with a behavioral trait that is, in essence, irreversible and in this chapter we explain our reasons for this belief.

THE NATURE—NURTURE CONTROVERSY

Psychologists have been arguing for years about the effects of genetics on behavior. Numerous prominent psychologists have argued that heredity determines behavior,

65

and that the environment is not a critical determinant. Other scientists have taken the position that all behavior is learned, and that your horse is not born with a propensity to behave in any given way. (The implications of this argument for the reader are obvious—if your horse is born with a certain personality then training techniques will in many cases be ineffective.) This whole issue has been coined the nature—nurture controversy and of all the issues over which behavioral scientists have disagreed, this one has probably been the most widely debated. It is our position that an artificial dichotomy has been created with genetic factors on one side and environmental factors on the other. It seems much more reasonable to assume that all behavior is affected by *both* hereditary factors and environmental variables. This is a theoretical stance that has been taken by numerous other investigators and Beach (1947) has stated that "It has long been apparent that a strict separation of the effects of inheritance from those of the individual's environment is impossible from a practical point of view and undesirable from a theoretical one." All too frequently, animal trainers have taken the position that behaviors resistant to training techniques are inbred. This is not usually true. Frequently, the reason the animal has not changed is simply because the correct behavior-change technique has not been utilized.

We do not mean to take the position that heredity does not influence behavior. Such an assertion would be unreasonable. Behavior is the product of an interaction between a physical system, made up of cells, muscles, etc., and the environment. The fact that these physical systems are largely determined by genetic factors means that heredity will influence behavior. But the nature of the interaction that takes place between the environment and the physical system is so complicated that it is often hard to tell how much of a role heredity really plays. The point we are trying to make is that an animal doesn't inherit behavior, but it does inherit those physiological systems that mediate behavior.

The complex manner in which physiological and environmental variables interact to produce behavior has been discussed by Kuo (1967). He emphasizes that the interaction between the organism and the environment takes place on both the overt behavioral level and on a physiological level and that these interactions result ". . . in a mutual modification of both the organism and the environment." In other words, the effects of the environment are such that they often result in a change in the physiology of the animal. On the other hand, a physiological change in the organism often seems to produce a change in the environment. These interactions become so complicated that it becomes almost impossible to figure out whether a behavior pattern is the result of environmental factors or genetic ones.

It would seem reasonable to speculate that hereditary factors play an important role in determining the biochemical constitution of an animal. Since a number of biochemicals have been linked to emotional behavior, it may well be that an animal's emotional makeup is influenced by genetic variables. Carlton (1969) for example, has taken the position that emotional behavior is mediated by chemical neurotransmitters that exist in the brain and he believes that imbalances in these chemicals may cause emotional disorders. Perhaps this is why drug therapy is useful in treating emotional problems such as depression and manic behavior in humans. Genetic factors may play an important role in determining whether this type of biochemical imbalance exists in a given organism. Just as heredity has been linked to depression and manic-depressive illness in humans, nervous problems may well be influenced by genetic variables in horses.

There has not been a great deal of research performed on the relationships that may exist between heredity and emotionality in the horse. This subject has been studied extensively in other species. Some behavioral psychologists have tried to find out whether heredity exerts an effect on the emotional behavior of rats. Hall (1941) and Searle (1949) discovered that much of the rat's emotional behavior is genetically influenced and they determined that the rat's emotional makeup played an important role in determining their performance on a wide range of learning tasks. Other scientists (Murphree and Dykman, 1965; Murphree, Dykman and Peters, 1967) have examined the role of genetic factors in determining the emotional behavior of pointer dogs. They used selective mating and line breeding techniques for a ten year period and successfully developed two strains of pointer dogs. One of these strains was called the A strain and it consisted of animals with relatively normal temperaments. Those animals that belonged to the B strain were high-strung to the point of being neurotic. The experimenters initially thought that they would have to breed several generations of dogs before a truly neurotic breed would develop. It was their hypothesis that the neurotic nature of these dogs would only become apparent when they were under extremely stressful conditions. As it turned out, it was much easier to breed a neurotic strain of dog than they had initially expected. They found that a neurotic breed could be developed over a single generation and this neurotic behavior was exhibited under all circumstances, not just stressful ones. As they put it, the dogs ". . . developed abnormal behavior spontaneously" (Murphree, *et al.*, 1967). These nervous dogs differed from normal animals in terms of many aspects of their emotional behavior. But there were two general factors that seemed to account for a great deal of their abnormal behavior—they were unusually fearful and timid.

The results of this experiment seemed to indicate that heredity exerted a great deal of influence upon the formation of emotional behavior. But, being good scientists, they realized that there was an alternative explanation. It was quite possible that the neurotic behavior was not due to genetics, but was instead due to the fact that the pups were raised by neurotic mothers. Perhaps the neurotic mothers made their offspring so insecure that they, too, became neurotic. In order to determine if this was the case, Murphree and his colleagues (Murphree and Newton, 1971) designed a clever experiment. They began by crossbreeding the normal dogs (A strain) with the neurotic dogs (B strain). In doing this, they were ensuring the fact that each puppy would have one neurotic parent. The critical factor was that half of the puppies had normal mothers and half of the puppies had neurotic mothers. They reasoned that if the puppies did, in fact, learn to be neurotic from their mothers that the pups raised by the normal mothers should also be normal. But, if the neurotic condition was caused by genetic factors, the pups should be neurotic anyway (because their fathers were from the neurotic strain). All of the animals in the experiment turned out to be equally neurotic, and the experimenters concluded that the neurotic behavior of their B strain was a result of genetic factors.

Exactly what does Murphree mean when he calls his dogs neurotic? He tested his animals using a number of different experimental procedures. The dogs' responses to people were assessed, their exploratory behavior and reactions to loud noises were tested and they were also tested on a number of different conditioning tasks. It was discovered that their behavior was characterized by timidity, fear of humans, a reduction of exploratory behavior and an exaggerated startle response to loud noises (Murphree, 1973). These dogs also were highly susceptible to mange and their neurotic condition began to develop at an age of two months and was grossly apparent by the time they were six months old.

The results of these experiments would seem to indicate that genetic variables exert a powerful influence upon the emotional reactivity of animals. Even more importantly, this emotional reactivity exerts a strong effect upon the performance of many tasks which you might want your horse to perform. Scott and Fuller (1965) subjected various breeds of dogs to numerous testing situations and found that some of the breeds displayed a much higher degree of emotionality than did others. Given their results, they concluded that the highly reactive animals had a very hard time on tasks in which they had to inhibit themselves. A highly reactive animal, for example, would have a hard time sitting still for even moderately long periods of time. Other dogs had very little difficulty sitting still even for very long periods of time.

It seems that emotional reactivity may be a result of genetic forces and the data indicates that this type of emotional reactivity affects performance on a wide variety of learning tasks. These findings contain grave implications for the horse owner. Obviously, the horse owner will require that his or her horse be able to inhibit itself in a wide variety of circumstances. It is important that fearfulness, timidity and emotional reactivity be assessed before the adult horses are bred. If a neurotic genetic component is present in the parents, there is a high probability that their offspring will exhibit similar behavioral conditions.

Up to this point, we have been discussing the effects of genetic variables upon temperament and emotional reactivity. But what about intelligence? Certainly the reader has heard that a highly intelligent mare is bound to give birth to an equally intelligent foal. But exactly what is intelligence? Usually when we talk about intelligence we are referring to an animal's performance on a particular task or series of tasks. The way that an animal performs on a task is affected by a wide range of different factors—the emotional state of the animal (as we have previously discussed), the environment and previous learning opportunities. Therefore, task performance reflects all of those variables as well as the one we intended to measure in the first place, which is intelligence. Some investigators have tested different breeds of animals on a wide variety of different tasks. They figured that if there is such a thing as a general factor of intelligence, then it should enable a given animal to perform superlatively on all tasks. As it turned out, this was not the case. It would seem that superior performance on a given task is more of a reflection of the animal's temperament, physical ability or previous learning than it is of the animal's intelligence. This conclusion has been supported by numerous comparative psychologists (Scott and Fuller, 1965; Fox, 1974). This is not to say that some individual animals are not gifted in that they can perform unusually well on a number of tasks. Our point is that given a normal emotional state and a competent trainer, your horse should be able to learn those tasks expected of him. All too frequently, though, the horse owner places the responsibility for her/his own teaching inadequacies upon his/her horse by calling it stupid. When the horse is having difficulty learning a simple task one of three problems is probably present: (1) the animal is emotionally upset or anxious, (2) inappropriate training techniques are being used or (3) the horse has learned things in the past that make learning on a new task more difficult. Blaming the horse's difficulties on low intelligence is nothing more than a cop-out.

HEREDITY AND TRAINING

We have discussed the possible effects of heredity upon the emotional makeup of an animal and it would seem that genetic influences are present. The question then becomes one of ascertaining the limitations that heredity may impose upon training. It is important to remember that although heredity affects emotional makeup, it does not determine how an animal will behave in a given situation. What happens is that genetic variables determine the *range of behaviors* that is possible for an animal in a given situation. In his theory of behavioral potentials, Kuo (1967) discusses a term he calls behavioral potentials. He defines this term as "... the enormous possibilities or potentialities of behavior patterns that each neonate possesses within the limits or range of the normal morphological structure of its species." In discussing behavioral potentials Kuo emphasizes that while an animal does not inherit behavioral predispositions, it is born with a certain physiological makeup that limits the range of behaviors it will be able to perform. By conceptualizing behavior in this manner, he is able to accept the role that heredity plays in determining the organism's physiology while retaining the notion that the animal is still able to behave in a wide variety of different ways. It is the physiological limitations which are inherited—*not the behaviors*.

Kuo (1967) has described a series of experiments that offer a stiff challenge to the way in which many of us think about genetics and heredity. Certainly most of us think of cats as being born with an instinct to pounce upon mice, rats, birds and other little animals. Few cat owners have had to train their cats to chase mice! But Kuo found that if kittens were raised in a well-controlled environment from the very moment they were born, then those cats would not be rat haters. How did he do this? Simple. He raised the cat with a baby rat and found that the two grew up to be best of friends. By utilizing different types of experimental procedures Kuo was successful in raising animals that behaved in ways that were quite peculiar. He raised cats that loved birds, kittens that were afraid of birds and dogs that were afraid of little white mice. What was the point of all this? Kuo simply wanted to demonstrate that animals are not born with innate personality predispositions. Every animal, your horse included, is capable of learning an incredibly wide range of behaviors.

We are attempting to convince the reader that his/her horse is not born with a given personality. Indeed, the type of personality which your horse develops is, to a large extent, up to you. As Kuo has emphasized, the range of possible behaviors which an animal can perform is extremely broad and is determined through the presence of a number of factors other than genetic ones. Often what happens is that a person observes his or her horse behaving in a certain manner under certain conditions and concludes that the observed behavior is an inborn personality characteristic of that animal. This observation soon becomes a self-fulfilling prophecy. Without realizing it, the horse owner does not provide the animal with opportunities to learn to behave differently. The reader must remember that behavior must be analyzed within the context of the enviornment in which it occurs. Just because your horse acts one way in one setting doesn't mean that it would act the same way in a different environment.

What are the other variables (besides genetic ones) which determine the range of behaviors which your horse will be able to perform? As we will see, early experience is an extremely important factor. Kuo has discussed the effects of the early environment and he has speculated that in the newborn infant there exists a remarkably wide range of behavioral potentials. With experience, however, this range of behavioral potentials tends to narrow and the animal is not capable of performing as many behaviors. Many behaviors which we think of as being inherited are actually behaviors learned during infancy. They appear to be inborn because they are so resistant to change. The reason these behaviors are not easily altered is not because of genetics, but because they were learned early in life and have been part of the animal's life for such a long time that the horse is not about to give them up. It is up to you, the horse owner, to provide your animal with the type of environment that will facilitate the development of a pleasing personality. Provide your young horse with a wide range of different experiences and be certain that it has many positive interactions with many different people. By doing so, you will maximize the probabilities of your horse becoming an adult who is gentle and friendly around people. If you are preparing your horse for competition, introduce its various facets at an early age. Do so in a way that is positive and fun. A little bit of reward at an early age will lead to the development of an animal that performs out of a love for performing—not because it feels it must. The type of personality that your horse develops is, to a large extent, up to you.

SUMMARY

The nature—nuture issue is an extraordinarily complex one. The evidence that we have reviewed indicates that genetic variables have potent effects upon an animal's physiological makeup and upon many aspects of its emotional behavior. It would seem that some symptoms of neurotic conditions (e.g., timidity, fearfulness) may be influenced by genetic factors. Breeders should carefully assess the behavior patterns of horses before mating. Despite all of this, an animal is usually capable of emitting a much wider range of behavior than the typical horse owner would expect. While hereditary factors set certain limits upon behavior, they do not usually determine the nature of an animal's personality or how it will behave in a given situation. It is important for the reader to remember that both heredity and environment affect behavior and the reader must capitalize on both of these factors. Many of those behaviors which we think are inborn are actually learned during infancy. By providing your horse with a broad range of positive experiences as a foal you will maximize the chances of it developing a pleasing personality.

CHAPTER 5

Development of Behavior

In this chapter we discuss the manner in which the horse's early experiences influence the development of its adult behavior. The point which we will repeatedly emphasize is that those experiences that the horse has during the first few months of life have a dramatic impact upon the development of its adult personality. Because there has been very little research performed on the behavioral development of horses, we will focus our discussion on work that has been done with other species and we will explain the implications of those studies for the horse owner. This chapter is an extremely important one, because much of your horse's behavior and general temperament is a result of the types of experiences it had when it was young. The horse owner should remember that many undesirable behaviors may be prevented through the proper management of the foal's early environment.

THE IMPORTANCE OF EARLY EXPERIENCE IN HUMANS

Theorists interested in explaining human behavior have long emphasized the importance of those experiences which

take place in early life. In his attempts to explain human behavior, Sigmund Freud speculated that during infancy the
child is particularly susceptible to psychological trauma. He
theorized that traumas which occur during early life lead to
the development of behavioral disorders which he called
neuroses, and he argued that if the child experienced difficulties during certain early developmental periods (he called
them psychosexual stages) he or she would develop certain
personality traits. Freud's emphasis upon the importance of
early experience is evidenced in his statement that ". . . the
very impressions which we have forgotten have nevertheless
left the deepest traces in our psychic life, and acted as determinants for our future development" (Freud, 1905).

Psychoanalytic theorists are not alone in their emphasis
upon the importance of early experience. Gardner Murphy
(1947) also paid a great deal of attention to the effects of
early experience when he formulated his theory of motiva-
tion. Murphy speculated that a child has an innate propensity
to respond to certain types of environmental stimuli in fairly
specific ways, and he reasoned that as the child matures it
responds to an increasingly narrow range of stimuli. According to this theory, the child develops a preference for those
stimuli with which he or she became familiar at an early age
and, as the child grows older, she or he is less likely to develop preferences that differ from those established during
infancy. Murphy calls this process canalisation, and it is
through this process that the general needs of the infant develop into the more specific needs that motivate adult behavior. This notion of canalisation serves to illustrate an
important developmental concept—that the range of behavior
that an organism is comfortable with narrows as the organism grows older. A young girl, for example, may feel that
she could respond to a given situation in a wide variety of
different ways, but once she grows older and gets some more
experience under her belt, she will probably feel that there
are a limited number of ways to appropriately deal with a

situation. As a rule, adults are not as flexible as infants because they have learned to deal with situations in specific ways.

The effects of early experience have also been emphasized in studies of intellectual processes. Piaget (1975) studied the intellectual development of the child and found that as the child progresses through developmental stages, he learns to respond in certain ways to certain stimuli and not to respond to others. According to Piaget's theory, the child must learn to perform certain cognitive (i.e., thinking) tasks during each developmental stage if he or she is to advance to the next one at which time more complex types of thinking tasks would be learned. Once again, we see that early experience is important in laying the foundations for adult behavior.

Many other investigators have also emphasized the important role that early experience plays in determining the psychological makeup of the adult human being. The examples we have offered illustrate the point that even in a creature as complex as the human being, early childhood experience can exert a profound influence upon the subsequent development of adult behavior patterns. In less complex organisms, such as the horse, early experience can play an even more important role. Although there has been little research done with horses, a general review of the literature dealing with the development of animal behavior should demonstrate that there are certain critical periods during infancy that are especially important in the development of the adult animal's personality. As we examine the data that have been collected from experiments utilizing rats, cats, apes, birds, sheep and goats, it will become apparent that early experiences are important in influencing the behavior of all members of the animal realm, as well as humankind's.

The Effects of Early Experience

When we address the notion that a horse's early experiences have a profound effect on its later development, it is possible to follow two different lines of reasoning. First, one could reason that early experiences are especially important by virtue of the fact that they occur before other experiences and thus they have a more dramatic impact. For example, a young man asking a young lady out for a date for the first time might be quite traumatized if she turns him down rudely. This unpleasant experience might even cause him to temporarily refrain from asking other women out for dates. On the other hand, if that man has the same experience ten years later, it is far less likely that he will be adversely affected. As he is more experienced, he can take the incident with a grain of salt and place it within the context of all of his heterosexual contacts. We see then that the same experience can have very different effects depending on when they happen in a life span. By following this line of reasoning, however, one assumes that the learning process itself (i.e., how information is biologically processed) is pretty much the same regardless of when it takes place.

There is some evidence suggesting that the learning which takes place during certain critical periods of early development actually occurs in a way much different from later learning. This means that it is especially important for the horse owner to make sure that his or her horse has the proper experiences during early life because what's learned during these experiences could conceivably be irreversible.

How could learning that takes place in early development be qualitatively different from learning which takes place in later life? After all, isn't all learning the same? Perhaps not. It is important to keep in mind that all learning is mediated by physiological systems (e.g., nerves, brain, central nervous system, etc.) and that a very young animal is physically different from older animals. It is quite possible that these physiological differences affect the way that things are learned. There is some experimental evidence which seems to indicate that early experiences have a profound effect on the manner in which the body's hormonal stress systems develop. This evidence is very important because these hormonal systems are involved in much of the adult horse's behavior. During a horse race, for example, these systems would play an important role in determining the horse's responses to environmental cues.

Levine (1967, 1972) is one of the scientists who has attempted to determine whether the experiences which an organism has during infancy affects the development of its physiological stress systems. He speculated that there might be a period of time during early life when handling and being comforted might actually enable an organism to learn what kinds of environmental stimulation are important and what kinds are not. He tested this hypothesis and found that this was indeed the case. To be more specific, he found that animals that were handled during early life showed higher levels of stress hormones than unhandled animals in situations where an unpleasant stimulus was introduced. When there was no aversive stimulation present, however, the man-handled animals had lower levels of stress hormones. In other words, when there really was something stressful introduced into the environment the stress systems of the unhandled animals did not really react all that strongly. This is not very adaptive. After all, during times of stress the animal needs to become aroused so that it can deal with the situation in some constructive manner. On the other hand, when there was nothing stressful present in the environment, the non-handled animals had higher levels of stress hormones. It would seem that the unhandled animals were always uptight regardless of whether there really was an external stress present. In a subsequent study, Levine (1967) concluded that his experiments ". . . continue to support the interpretation that the absence of extrinsic stimulation in infancy results in an increase in the subject's susceptibility to emotional disturbance," and that ". . . the resulting emotional disturbance is sufficiently intense to interfere with subsequent adaptive behavior.'' These experiments would seem to indicate that the stimulation which an animal receives when it is very young actually affects the manner in which the animal's hormonal stress system develops and also affects the organization of adult behavior patterns.

Learning during infancy might differ from adult learning in another way. Evidence suggests that young animals are genetically preprogrammed to learn certain things at certain times in their lives. It is possible that animals are biologically prepared to learn some things when they are young that they cannot learn or unlearn as they grow older. Probably the most dramatic illustration of this type of learning is a phenomenon called imprinting. The term imprinting was first introduced by Konrad Lorenz (who shared a Nobel Prize for this discovery). Lorenz (1970) found that young birds don't instinctively recognize members of their own species, but they instinctively follow the first moving object they encounter during a certain critical period in early life. Once the bird has reached this critical age, it will instinctively follow the first moving object it encounters. It will form a lasting emotional attachment to that object and also to other members of that object's species. Thus, if the young bird reaches this critical time period and sees a human being moving around its nest, it will follow that individual and, over time, will become attached to that person and to other human beings as well. Paradoxically, the same bird may be quite *dis*interested in interacting with other birds! While this may seem somewhat peculiar to the reader, one must remember that this imprinting mechanism is usually well suited for the young bird and for the species as a whole. After all, the young bird typically encounters members of its own species during this critical time period and becomes emotionally attached to them. Mother Nature did not take into account the possibility that scientists might intervene and find out that the young birds could be imprinted to members of other species.

It is important to remember that this imprinting process only occurs during a certain critical time period and that once the bird has reached this critical age it is genetically preprogrammed to follow a moving object. Once this critical time period has passed, imprinting will not occur. This theoretical stance differs from the position taken by many behavioral psychologists (e.g., B. F. Skinner) who stress that all learning is the result of rewards and punishments and that genetic factors are not involved. Lorenz makes his position quite clear in his book *Studies in Animal and Human Behavior* (1970):

> The most important result of this investigation of instinctive behavior patterns (is) the fact that not all acquired behavior can be equated with experience and that not all processes of acquisition can be equated with learning. We have seen that in many cases the object appropriate to innately determined instinctive behavior patterns is not instinctively recognized as such, but that regardless of the object acquired through a quite specific process, it has nothing to do with learning.

Thus it becomes apparent that Lorenz views the imprinting process as being totally irreversible and that concepts usually regarded as being basic to all learning processes, such as reinforcement, are quite irrelevant to the imprinting process. The phenomenon of imprinting demonstrates the fact that many of those experiences that occur during infancy have dramatic and long-lasting effects that persist long into adult life. In addition, it would seem that there are certain critical periods during which the animal is biologically prepared to learn certain associations. In Lorenz's studies learning either occurred during these critical periods or it did not occur at all.

This phenomenon of developing emotional attachments at an early age has been evidenced in other species as well. Stanley and Elliott (1962) have demonstrated that dogs seem to develop intense emotional attachments during early life and those attachments seem similar to those observed in Lorenz's birds. In their experiment, Stanley and Elliott separated young pups from their mothers when the pups were six weeks old. After the pups were separated from their mothers their only contact with other organisms was with the human experimenters. The pups were never fed by the experimenters and the experimenters took special care not to pet or come into any kind of physical contact with the young pups. The experimenters would possibly sit in a chair in the pup's cage for a short period of time on a daily basis. Despite the lack of reinforcement and the lack of physical contact between the pups and the people, all of the pups developed strong emotional attachments to the experimenters. This study would seem to demonstrate that the learning of emotional bonds takes place early in the pup's life and Scott and Fuller (1965) concluded that this type of early learning constitutes a period of socialization which is largely independent of outside experiences.

Whether this type of learning is innate or more subtly different from adult learning is probably not of great importance to the reader who is more interested in practical applications and training implications. What is important to horse owners is the fact that there is a relatively brief period of time during early life in which animals develop emotional attachments. This period may be called a socialization period and it would seem that the part of an animal's personality that makes it compatible with people develops during this time period. This issue is relevant to the horse owner. If a horse does not develop attachments to people during this socialization period, the horse may become anxious around people and will not learn tasks as efficiently as it would were it more relaxed. In addition, it would probably require an inordinately large amount of effort and time to correct for that personality deficit. Some investigators, in fact, have taken the position that if an animal does not develop these attachments during early life then it will be impossible to learn them later on. Other studies, however, have shown that this is not necessarily the case. Woolpy and Ginsberg (1967) performed an experiment with adult wolves that had never before come into contact with humans. They wanted to find out how long it would take to get unsolicited wolves used to being around people. The experimenters began by placing these unsolicited wolves in individual cages and then they would sit quietly in a corner in the cage for 10 to 20 minutes on a daily basis. They repeated this procedure for several months. At first, the wolves would frantically try to escape from the cage and they would usually cower in the corner opposite the experimenter and shake and urinate uncontrollably. The wolves remained desperately afraid of the two men for about thirty days. Then, slowly but surely, the wolves became less anxious and silently sat as far as possible from the experimenter and quietly watched his every movement. But if the man in the cage made a sudden movement, the wolf would regress to its previous highly anxious state and would frantically try to escape from the cage. The state of affairs lasted several months until finally the wolves allowed the person in the cage to approach and even make physical contact. During this period the wolves eventually reached the point at which they would investigate the experimenter by rubbing against him and chewing on his clothing. If the experimenter made a sudden movement, however, the wolves either attacked him or would try to escape from the cage. The wolf would then remain fearful for several weeks. (Needless to say, this experiment required experimenters that were very brave.) If no such setback occurred, the wolves would ultimately become socialized to the experimenters and would generalize these effects to other people. We see, then, that the absence of certain early experiences does not always result in deficits that are completely irreversible. But the fact remains that it took the adult wolves months and months to become comfortable with people when they could have developed the same sort of attachments over a period of a few short weeks when they were pups.

Once again we see that if an animal is to be relaxed with a certain species it is best that the animal be socialized to that species at quite a young age. As we have previously emphasized, early experiences exert a profound effect on the adult animal's ability to deal with training regimens and their ability to learn certain tasks. The manner in which the lack of positive social experiences may severely disrupt a wider range of adult behavior patterns has been demonstrated by Seitz (1959) with cats and Harlow (1962a, 1962b) with apes. Both of these studies have clear-cut implications for the horse owner.

Seitz (1959) separated kittens from their mothers at either two, six or twelve weeks of age and then proceeded to rear them in individual cages. He waited until they were nine months old and then tested them with a wide variety of behavioral tests designed to assess their general behavior, learning ability, reactions to stress and the manner in which they dealt with frustration. Seitz discovered that those animals that were seperated earlier in life were (1) most anxious in new situations, (2) more susceptible to conflict, (3) more aggressive, (4) more persistent (but also more disorganized when they attempted to secure food when hungry and frustrated), (5) slower learners and (6) more fearful of other cats and people. The experimenter concluded that traumatic experiences which occur during early life ". . . have persistent effects upon adult behavior, lasting throughout the lifetime of the animal," and Seitz argues that these early traumas will have detrimental effects upon practically all adult behavior.

The work of Seitz indicates that a disruption of an animal's early life patterns will result in severe emotional disturbances later in life. This possibility seems even more likely given the work of Harry Harlow, who studied the development of emotional behavior in apes. Harlow (1962a, 1962b) separated monkeys from their mothers shortly after they were born. In a cleverly designed experiment, Harlow replaced the mother monkeys with what he called surrogate mothers. These surrogate mothers were actually cylindrical objects that were designed to be close to the actual size and shape of the real mother monkeys. They were made either of terry cloth (so that they would be cuddly) or of wire. Both the cloth and wire surrogate mothers were constructed with feeding bottles attached to them so that the young apes would nurse from them. The only real difference between the cloth and wire mothers was in their appearance and, more importantly, in the way they felt when the young monkeys tried to hold them. Half the baby monkeys were assigned to the terry cloth mothers while the other half were assigned to the mothers made of wire mesh. Thus this experiment was designed to see if it really is important for the young animals to have something warm and cuddly to hold onto (as they would have with their own mothers).

The results of these experiments were quite astounding. The baby apes that were raised with the cloth mothers actually became attached to them in much the same way that they would have become attached to real mothers. If the monkeys were frightened, they would run to their cloth mothers and cling to them until they had settled down. The monkeys that had been raised with wire mothers behaved much differently, and they did not evince any sort of attachment to their surrogate mothers. While the monkeys raised with the cloth mothers actually seemed to receive some sort of emotional comfort by being around them, the other apes were indifferent to their wire surrogate mothers. These monkeys, if frightened, would frantically run about their cage and rock back and forth in a convulsive manner. Harlow (1962a) stated that ". . . such activities closely resemble the autistic behavior seen frequently among neglected children in and out of institutions." He followed up this dramatic experiment with another study in which he raised one pair of infant monkeys together from 90 days of age and raised eight other baby monkeys with the same cloth surrogate mothers during the same time period. Two other monkeys were raised in total isolation. The eight monkeys raised with cloth mothers developed extremely strong emotional attachments to them and, by and large, their emotional development was fairly normal. The other two groups did not fare so well. The two infant monkeys that had been raised together, but had been deprived of the type of contact comfort they might have received from their real mothers, developed serious emotional problems and had much difficulty getting along with other apes. The two young monkeys that had been raised in complete isolation were extremely deviant and they were described as being in a catatonic state. That is, instead of interacting with other monkeys they would simply lie immobile in their cage much like hospitalized catatonic schizophrenics will sit in chairs for days at a time without showing any signs of movements or interest in their environment.

All of the experimental evidence we have reviewed indicates that the first few months of life are important determinants of adult behavior. If the normal developmental sequences of animals are disrupted, they will probably grow up to be anxious and difficult to train. When more serious infantile traumas occur, the adult animal may actually suffer from severe emotional disturbances (resembling schizophrenic symptoms). Unfortunately, there have been no experimental studies of acceptable quality performed with horses, but since the studies reviewed have involved a wide variety of different species, and because the results have all been very similar, there is little reason to think that their findings may not be generalized to horses. It is extremely unlikely that the behavior of the horse would develop in a manner so totally different from other animals. Indeed, these developmental phenomena have been observed in animals ranging from young birds (Lorenz, 1970), to young dogs (Stanley & Elliot, 1962), to humans (Freud, 1905). Now we will look at how these data might affect the manner in which you raise your horse, and we will look more specifically at the early development of the horse.

THE EARLY DEVELOPMENT OF THE HORSE

After a gestation period of approximately 320 to 355 days, the mare gives birth to the foal. This usually occurs within a few hours after midnight (Vaura, 1979). The newborn foal is a rather fragile and uncoordinated beast that is closely watched and protected by its mother. Like other ungulates, the foal is precocious in its behavioral development. Its sensory and motor systems are functional shortly after birth and the foal displays adult-like behavior patterns rather quickly. The implications of the precocious nature of the newborn foal are very important. In many other animals, the imprinting or socialization process does not begin for several weeks. But, because the foal is born with functional sensory and motor systems, the socialization process takes place almost immediately. This socialization period lasts little more than one week, and the foal forms an extremely close relationship with its mother during this period. It is important that this imprinting period be uninterrupted. The evidence which we have previously reviewed indicates that isolating the newborn may lead to the development of undesirable behavioral states in the adult animal.

Because the young foal is quite fragile, it stays close to its mother for the first few days of life. Soon, however, it begins to become more mobile and it starts to explore its environment more actively. The foal nurses several times an hour, usually for periods of three to four minutes, and it displays some sexual behavior within the first few weeks of life (Vaura, 1979). The foal shows some rudimentary territorial behavior as it establishes scent-posts with urine, becoming increasingly mobile at a very young age.

Mother Nature has provided the foal with numerous opportunities to engage in important learning experiences with other members of the herd. It is important that the foal be given the opportunity to interact with other horses so that these learning experiences may take place. The normal sexual behavior (e.g., courting) that the foal engages in with his herd mates are necessary for the establishment of normal adult sexual behavior, and it has been experimentally demonstrated with other species that young animals deprived of sexual experiences are often unable to mate as adults (Beach, 1968).

If the horse is to be truly comfortable with humans, it is important that it be allowed to interact with humans at an early age. During the period of intense imprinting that takes place in the first week of life, the foal and its mother should be left alone so that the imprinting process may naturally emerge. After this period the mother will become less protective of the foal, and the owner may introduce him or herself to the animal on a regular basis. It is important that the foal learn that its herd consists of people as well as horses. The person should provide some contact comfort to the foal, but should be careful not to disrupt the foal's interactions with other horses. The owner needs to blend in with the herd without disrupting it. The rearing conditions should be as natural as possible, while allowing the horse to become partially socialized to humans. If the horse is not allowed to become socialized to members of its own species, the development of many desirable adult behavior patterns may be impeded and the horse may not perform adequately as an adult. The key is to achieve a happy medium in which a variety of socialization experiences are available to the horse.

As we have previously stated, the occurrence of trauma during infancy may lead to the development of behavior disorders as an adult. The first few weeks are the most important weeks of the horse's life and it is during this period that much of its personality is determined. Great care must be taken to make sure that the animal is not traumatized and that relatively positive horse-to-horse and person-to-person interactions take place. While no empirical research has been performed on the effects of different trauma on the behavioral development of the horse, it is our educated guess that many of the behavioral deficits present in adult horses are the result of deficits or trauma present during the horse's first few weeks of life.

CHAPTER 6

Learning Theory, Principles of Learning, and Equine Behavior Control

Psychology is a very diverse field subsuming the study of many aspects of behavior. Earlier we discussed one area of psychology, comparative psychology, and we have written much of this book from a comparative psychology frame of reference. Another major branch of psychology important to the horse owner is the psychology of learning.

What is learning? How do we know when an organism has learned something? How do we measure learning? Before we can attempt to answer these three questions, let us consider the act of learning first. Have you ever seen an animal or a person learn something? If you answer yes, what did you see? Have you ever tried to teach a child, another person or an animal to perform some behavior? If you have, what did you look for to determine whether that organism learned what you taught? How well were the things you taught learned?

As you think about those things, let's consider an example. Frost, a hungry three-year-old quarter horse, is placed in a new pen. His new nighttime pen is only about ten feet away from a luscious bag of oats left in the barn. Now, let's get out of sight and watch. Frost ambles around the pen at first, exploring his new surroundings, when he smells and sees those luscious oats. He tries walking toward them but is thwarted by the fence. He then walks up and down the fence trying a push here and a push there on the fence when, accidentally, he pushes on the board which holds the gate shut. As he does so, the board falls away and the gate opens. Frost then gleefully walks out of the gate and over to the oats. Our question is: Did Frost learn anything?

All we saw was Frost pushing the fence until he accidentally hit the right spot. Then we saw him get out and go eat. From what we saw, we could not say one way or the other if Frost learned anything. How can we tell if he did learn something? Well, let's put him back in the pen and watch once more. Let's also assume that he's still hungry. As Frost is put back into the pen we watch him once more. This time he doesn't beat around the bush. He goes directly to the board which he pushed to get out the last time and pushes once more. As he does so, he goes to the oats once more. Do we now know that Frost has learned something?

The example of Frost was used to illustrate one very important fact about learning. We can never see learning occur directly whether in a horse or in a human. Think about it. You cannot *see* into an organism's brain to see whether or not learning has occurred. Learning can only be inferred from the observation of behavior. We infer that Frost learned something because the second time we placed him in the pen he went directly to the right board, pushed it and got out, whereas the first time he fumbled around all over the fence. We could not see him learn—we could only see the result of his learning. We use behavior—performance if you prefer—to assess learning. For students, we ask that they read some material and we then test them on the material. The test scores are measures of performance which are then used to infer learning.

Learning is defined by the consensus as a relatively permanent change in behavior brought about by an organism's experience with the environment. (This definition excludes changes in behavior that are the results of illness, fatigue or chemical change. Such things may change behavior, but the behavior is not being changed by experience, the behavior is being changed by altering the internal state of the animal.) Learning is measured by assessing behavior and we know we have taught something when we have changed an organism's behavior. This is very important when you're trying to figure out how to teach an animal or control its behavior.

For you to become a proficient animal trainer, a modifier of equine behavior, it is necessary for you to see how different kinds of experiences affect animals. Put another way, you need to know how different environments affect animals in different ways. But even before we get to that, we should define the term environment.

An organism's environment consists of all those things perceived by the organism. This includes stimuli that can be tasted, smelled, touched, heard or seen. It includes things external to the organism, such as sounds and sights around it, and also things which are internal, such as feelings of hunger or the feel of muscles moving in a certain way. Only those things that the organism perceives are actually a part of the environment. A good example would be driving through a stop sign that you don't see. You go right through the intersection because if you don't see the sign it is just as though it were not there. Things that are present but not perceived may just as well not be there as far as the organism's behavior is concerned.

These perceptions are called stimuli. There are five types of stimuli and each type has a different effect on behavior. We should briefly note that the perception of stimuli must be considered in context. That is, a stimulus may be very large (a barn) or very small (one splinter on the side of a barn). Both of these must be seen in context. The barn will be small when viewed from a distance. Humans, for example, may respond to a huge semi-tractor trailer truck as *one* stimulus (when trying to pass one) or they may respond to one *bolt* on the truck as a stimulus (when changing the tire on the truck, each lug nut is perceived).

Neutral stimuli are the most common of all stimuli. Neutral stimuli are those stimuli perceived by an organism but which do not affect its behavior. Neutral stimuli for a horse may include the sound of machinery in a field a few hundred yards away, the grain pattern on a board, the pattern on the shirt you wear and so on. A horse can perceive (and probably does) all these stimuli but they are not likely to affect its behavior in any perceptible way. While neutral stimuli have no direct effect on behavior they do form a pool of stimuli from which other kinds of stimuli are formed.

Reinforcing stimuli are those stimuli that strengthen behavior. Reinforcers are not synonymous with rewards. Rewards are attempts to strengthen behavior (and as we know, they may or may not accomplish this). By definition, reinforcers *do* strengthen behavior. We determine which stimuli are reinforcers by observing their effects. If stimuli strengthen behavior, they are reinforcers. It does not matter what the stimulus looks like, tastes like, smells like, feels like or what we intend to do with it. All that matters is what the stimulus does. It is vitally important that you understand that it is the *effect* of the stimuli that matters, not other factors.

Reinforcers categorized as primary (food, water, air, rest, sexual stimulation and affection) are those stimuli which are innately reinforcing due to the biological nature of the organism. These kinds of reinforcers are reinforcing to a horse given the horse's biological needs. How powerful an effect such stimuli have on the behavior of an organism depends on many things—how hungry the horse is (food is not very effective when the horse is not hungry), how thirsty, how tired or how uncomfortable. If, for example, we intend to use food as a reinforcer in a training program, we ought to make sure that the horse is at least somewhat hungry.

There are also secondary reinforcers. Secondary reinforcers are stimuli that started out as neutral stimuli and through association with primary reinforcers have gained some of the value of the primary reinforcers. Secondary reinforcers are not necessary for biological survival. Stimuli such as the sounds "good boy," "good girl," a pat on the flank, a place (a special pen may be a reinforcing place for a horse) and so on, acquire their ability to strengthen behaviors because they have been associated with primary reinforcers. In this way, when you pair a handful of oats over and over with the sounds "good boy," you are literally teaching the horse that the sounds "good boy" have some of the value of the oats. Eventually, "good boy" will come to have the ability to strengthen behavior by itself.

We can also categorize reinforcers as positive and negative reinforcers. Simply stated, positive reinforcers follow behavior and strengthen the behavior they follow. A horse exhibits a behavior you want to strengthen and you follow the behavior with "good girl" and a pat on the flank. If the behavior is strengthened, you have administered positive reinforcement. (Please note that the word positive does not refer to positive behaviors, positive feelings or positive anything. We did not invent the phrase and we feel a more descriptive term could be employed to refer solely to a stimulus that strengthens a behavior it follows.)

Negative reinforcement refers to escape and avoidance behaviors. A negative reinforcer is a stimulus that, when removed by a behavior, strengthens that behavior. If a horse is being plagued by a big horsefly, the horse may try several things to get rid of the fly. Suppose a horse rids itself of a horsefly (a highly irritating stimulus) by galloping off into a field for several hundred yards. The horse has escaped from the horsefly by running and, if running behavior in the presence of horseflies has been increased, then we have seen an example of negative reinforcement. Any time escape from a stimulus is successful and the escape behavior is strengthened, we have an example of negative reinforcement. Avoidance is highly similar to escape. This time, if a horse successfully avoids a noxious stimulus with some behavior then that avoidance behavior is strengthened and we have witnessed negative reinforcement. Obviously, before avoidance behavior can occur an instance of escape behavior must have occurred for that stimulus first.

Reinforcing stimuli form the largest part of our behavioral change arsenal. The proper use of reinforcers allows us to do many things to change the behavior of organisms. There are, however, three other kinds of stimuli you should know about in order to make you the complete equine behavior modifier.

Punishing stimuli are those stimuli that weaken the behaviors they follow. Punishers are exactly the opposite of positive reinforcers. They may either be innate (usually physical discomfort) or learned (a particular tone of voice). Punishers are not defined by what they look like, feel like or what we intend them to be. They are defined solely by the effect they have on behavior. The statement "I tried punishment and it didn't work," is nonsense. Punishment, by definition, works. If you apply a stimulus to an organism and it does not weaken behavior, it is not punishment.

Eliciting stimuli are those stimuli that bring forth (cause, elicit) an involuntary reflex. These stimuli may be unlearned (a bug flying in the eye causes the reflex of blinking) or learned (if we were to sound a buzzer and administer an electric shock over and over, the buzzer itself would eventually cause the same reflex the shock originally caused). Involuntary behaviors are really not of great importance to modifiers of equine behavior. We mention them only because you are apt to encounter them and because the common conception of behavioral psychologists is that we go around conditioning reflexes.

Discriminative stimuli are far more important to us than eliciting stimuli. Discriminative stimuli are signposts in the enviornment that an organism reads and to which it responds appropriately. Discriminative stimuli start out as neutral stimuli and they become signposts by being paired with the reinforcement for specific behaviors in their presence. A trick horse, for example, that responds to the command "up" by raising its front legs has learned a discriminative stimulus for leg-raising behavior. Horses learn that some stimuli behaviors will be reinforced while others will not. Much of your training will be based on teaching discriminative stimuli to your horse.

SHAPING

Now that we have briefly identified the five kinds of stimuli that make up the enviornment, how do we describe the process of teaching behaviors to horses? Teaching new behaviors is a process psychologists frequently refer to as *shaping*. Shaping is the reinforcement of successive approximations of a goal behavior until we have formed and fixed the goal behavior into an organism's repertoire of behaviors. The shaping process will best make sense if we present an example of how behaviors may be shaped.

Suppose we have set up an experimental pen for a horse, Old Bullett, and we are about the business of shaping a new behavior. Old Bullett has never been in such a pen before. It is large enough for him to move around in comfortably (30 × 30). At one end of the pen is a rectangular light fixture which we may turn on and off as we desire by pushing a button on a console we have several feet away from the pen. On the opposite side of the pen is a food dispenser so constructed as to allow us to dispense pellets of food whenever we want to by pushing another button on our console. There is also a lever under the light which Old Bullet can depress by nuzzling it. We have attached this lever to an automatic counting device so that we can accurately keep track of Old Bullet's lever-pressing behavior. We will also assume that Old Bullet is in good health and that all his needs have been met with the exception of food. Bullet is hungry. To sum up, we have a healthy, hungry horse in a novel environment that we can control to some extent.

Now, as we settle back to watch Old Bullet, we decide to teach (shape) him to depress the lever when the light is turned on. This is not a difficult behavior to teach but it will take time. We'll allow Old Bullet several moments to become acclimated to the pen and then we'll decide to give him a pellet of food the first time he approaches the lever. Old Bullet, after quite a bit of walking around, finally approaches the lever and when he gets as close to it as we think he will, we dispense our food pellet. Old Bullet hears the noise and sees the food and walks over and hungrily gobbles up the pellet. Now we wait once more until Old Bullet once again approaches the lever. When he does, we give him another pellet of food. Now, before we give him the third pellet, we'll wait until he approaches the lever closer than before. We may need to wait several moments, but as soon as he does move closer than before, we hit our food dispenser button and give him another pellet. Over the course of the next couple of hours, we gradually shape Old Bullet's behavior, getting him to come closer and closer to the lever before we reinforce. Finally, we get him walking right up to the lever. Our next step is to get him to move his head to the lever until he actually depresses it.

Again, we wait. Old Bullet walks up to the lever, expecting reinforcement, but we wait until he makes any movement with his head toward the lever. As soon as he does so, we dispense a pellet of food. We continue this process until we get him to actually touch the lever with his muzzle. Now we make him exert pressure on the lever. As soon as he does so, we dispense still another pellet. A few moves from here and we have him pushing the lever, turning and walking over to his new pellet. We have successfully shaped his lever-pushing behavior. How do we now get him to respond to the lever only when the light is on? Well, this process, known as *discrimination*, bears closer examination.

Discrimination is the term we use for a process where an organism can determine when certain behaviors should occur. Literally, it is the ability to tell the difference between stimuli and behave appropriately in their presence. This whole business is based on the discriminative stimuli we talked about earlier. When reinforcement for a behavior always occurs in the presence of a specific stimulus and never occurs in its absence, organisms soon learn, through trial and error, when to behave a certain way and when not.

To get back to Old Bullet, all we have to do is turn the light on and reinforce him for the correct behavior when the light is on but never reinforce him when the light is off. If Old Bullet stays hungry for a while, we can just turn the light on and off, reinforcing him and not reinforcing him until we have him responding only when the light is on. If we want to get fancy and do something like the tricks we see animal trainers use, we can cut a stencil which spells out "Push the lever" and place this over the light. Since Bullet is responding to the light anyhow, all we have to do is continue to reinforce him for his lever-pushing behavior when the light is on. Now, it will look like Bullet is reading the sign and responding appropriately.

Depending on lots of things—our precision in running this shaping process, how fatigued Old Bullet becomes, how hungry Old Bullet is and so on—we could cut a second stencil saying "Do not press" and add this to our system so that half the time the light comes on and flashes "Do not press." If we reinforce him for lever pressing for our "Press the lever'' sign and never reinforce him when it says ''Do not press'' we could probably get him to make this discrimination. Such training appears to result in reading behavior.

Generalization

Generalization is a term applied to both stimulus and response. *Response generalization* is the phenomena we see when we train an organism to perform one specific behavior and, through this training, we also increase similar behaviors. This is easy to see in children. If a small child is reinforced for saying ''Hi,'' we are more likely to hear that child saying similar things, like ''Bye.'' In horses, if we reinforce lever-pushing behavior, we are also likely to strengthen similar behaviors—fence-pushing behavior and the like.

Stimulus generalization is the phenomena we see when we have trained an organism to emit a response in the presence of a certain discriminative stimulus and the organism also performs this behavior in the presence of similar but different discriminative stimuli.

When one of the writers was growing up on a farm, he had made it a practice to blow a novelty horn (too-da-de-da-de-too repeated several times) as he drove up to the barn to put out feed for the horses. It did not take long for the horses in the pasture to come running when they heard this horn. For a long time, however, they also ran to the barn anytime a similar noise was made. They generalized across stimuli.

Schedules of Reinforcement

One of the factors that strongly affects learning and maintenance of behavior is a schedule of *reinforcement*. A schedule of reinforcement is, as the term indicates, the schedule whereby a certain behavior is reinforced. Schedules of reinforcement is a topic to which several books and dozens of articles are devoted yearly. We don't need to be highly technical in our approach to reinforcement schedules as it is unlikely that you will have need for any of the more esoteric ones. It is important, though, that you see that new behaviors are best learned on a one-for-one schedule of reinforcement: one behavior—one reinforcer. This is the easiest and most efficient way of teaching a new behavior. There are all kinds of pitfalls in training if you do not follow this prescription. A one-for-one schedule is by far the best for training new behaviors.

There is a problem, though. Once you have taught a new behavior to a horse and the horse is performing it appropriately in the presence of the appropriate discriminative stimulus, you will not want to be tied to a one-for-one schedule of reinforcement. There are going to be times when you will want your horse to perform a behavior for which you cannot provide reinforcement. This kind of problem can be resolved by a procedure we call schedule stretching. Schedule stretching amounts to figuring that once a behavior is well established on a one-for-one basis, you may then begin to gradually withdraw some of the reinforcers for that behavior and still maintain it at the same high level of occurrence.

A couple of examples will help us illustrate. Let's use a very common example involving human beings. Suppose we want to teach a small child to say "thank you" after every adult behavior that results in the child's receiving some object. We start by performing the kind of shaping procedure we just described until we have the child saying "thank you" at the appropriate instance. We will assume that we have been using praise as the reinforcer for this behavior. Now although we want the behavior to continue to occur, we also know that we cannot possibly continue to reinforce this behavior indefinitely. In fact, we eventually want this behavior to occur without the need for frequent reinforcement. What we would do to stretch this schedule of reinforcement is to begin to leave out a reinforcer now and then and over a period of several days or weeks, maintaining the behavior by providing a reinforcer every so often. You move from one-for-one to one-for-two to one-for-ten and so forth.

The same process may be used with horses. Any time a behavior is fairly well fixed into a horse's behavioral repertoire by shaping, you can begin to stretch the schedule. Old Bullet, for example, could have his lever-pressing behavior gradually stretched from a one-for-one schedule to a highly infrequent schedule by merely leaving out a reinforcer now and then and gradually increasing the number of behaviors between reinforcers so that he would respond, say, 50 times between reinforcers.

It is possible to maintain some equine behaviors on infrequent schedules of reinforcement as low as one reinforcer for every 200 behaviors. Obviously a well-trained horse is an animal that performs the behaviors we want with a minimal amount of reinforcement.

Internalized Reinforcement

We can frequently observe animals that repeatedly perform behaviors in the absence of any kind of reinforcement. A horse, for example, may always respond to a person's spoken command for some behavior without receiving any apparent form of reinforcement for that behavior. This phenomenon is best accounted for by what is referred to as *internalized reinforcement*. Internalized reinforcement occurs when some behaviors, after often being paired with external reinforcement, become reinforcing in and of themselves. The activity has literally become a secondary reinforcer.

We can see such phenomena among people almost anywhere we look. Why do people play tennis? Think about it.

Playing tennis makes you tired, sore, hot, sweaty and frequently grumpy. Why, digging a hole in the ground and filling it back up again will do the same thing and you don't have to go the expense of buying a racquet or tennis outfits. How about driving golf balls? Some people will spend hour after solitary hour driving golf balls off a tee with no visible source of reinforcement. We can obtain similar physical benefits by chopping firewood. These kinds of activities have acquired reinforcing properties in and of themselves for those people who participate in them. These behaviors have been associated with many, many kinds of reinforcers—winning competitions, social approval and so on. Eventually people engage in such behaviors because the behaviors alone are enough reinforcement to continue.

Horses, too, learn some behaviors in this way. The specific behaviors, of course, depend on the horse and its history of reinforcement. We are aware of one old mare that persisted in shaking hands, a trick she learned when less than two years old, even though the owner had long since stopped reinforcing the behavior by grasping the hoof or even making any comment. Evidently this behavior paid off so well early in this mare's reinforcement history that six years later she continued to perform the behavior just because she liked it.

Extinction

Extinction occurs when a behavior stops appearing in an organism's repertoire of behaviors. There will be occasions when you will want to have a horse unlearn some behaviors. There are three ways in which extinction can be made to occur: (1) remove all reinforcement for that behavior; (2) replace reinforcing consequences with punishing consequences for the behavior you wish to extinguish; (3) counter-condition the animal. As unlearning inappropriate behaviors is as important as learning new ones in many cases, we shall examine these three techniques in detail.

Removing Reinforcement. The simplest (and most emotionally pleasing for us) way of extinguishing behaviors is to remove the reinforcing consequences of that behavior. To do this it is necessary first of all to observe the behavior extensively and find out what consequences are, in fact, the reinforcers.

To do this, observe the inappropriate behavior carefully. What are the consequences to the horse of the behaviors it emits? Whatever the consequences are, you must remember that some or all of the consequences are reinforcing (after all, they are maintaining the behavior). Second, remove these consequences altogether if possible. This process will extinguish most inappropriate behaviors. There are a couple of things you need to know about this business before you just jump into it. Things always get worse before they get better. A review of the literature on extinction reveals that behaviors that have obtained reinforcement and are then placed on extinction schedules (to have their reinforcement removed) tend to increase considerably before they start to decrease. Think about what happens when you drop coins into a soft drink machine and the coins slide right out again. Do you immediately stop and walk away from the machine? Not likely. When reinforcement is removed (a bottle of pop does not appear) then behavior tends to increase (coin-inserting behavior is repeated several times with the expectation that the reinforcement will surely be obtained sooner or later). When reinforcement is removed for a horse's behavior it too expects that if it just continues the behavior the reinforcement will arrive sooner or later.

Another thing to keep in mind is that reinforcement must be withdrawn absolutely for the behavior you wish to extinguish. If you slip up and allow a reinforcer to appear for the inappropriate behavior, even very rarely, what you are doing, in effect, is stretching the schedule of reinforcement and making the behavior even more resistant to extinction. The moral of this story is do not try to extinguish a behavior by withdrawing reinforcement unless you can withdraw it completely.

Punishing Inappropriate Behaviors. There will be times when you just cannot effectively remove the reinforcers for some behavior you want to extinguish. One alternative is to systematically punish the behavior while trying to remove the reinforcing consequences of the behavior at the same time. This process is fairly simple, conceptually. You merely identify a punishing stimulus for the horse and see that it is administered immediately after the inappropriate behavior. You will have to do the same kind of analysis we described earlier to determine which reinforcers are maintaining the inappropriate behavior. These reinforcers should be removed to the greatest extent possible.

This process sounds simple but it has some drawbacks. The most obvious drawback is that punishment is aversive for the horse and it is aversive for the person who administers it. The horse and the human typically feel much better when punishment is not used. Punishment also has side effects, usually in the form of emotional reactions—agitation, anger, distrust and fear. Punishment, when too severe or inconsistent, can literally make the person administering the punishment the stimulus that elicits a fear-response in the horse. What we are saying here and what will be re-emphasized is the idea that punishment must be very, very carefully administered.

A third concern is the fact that when reinforcers cannot be effectively withdrawn, they compete with the punishers. The horse will receive two consequences for a behavior, a punishing consequence and a reinforcing consequence. If the reinforcer is powerful enough, the horse will continue with the inappropriate behavior in spite of the punishment. The only effect of punishment in such situations is to bring about undesirable side effects as described above. So the punishment must be more powerful than the reinforcer for this process to be effective. You must also be very careful not to select a punishment which is too powerful or you will not get unlearning—you will only get a fear and anxiety response. More about this in Chapter 7.

Overall, the use of punishment to extinguish an inappropriate behavior is a last resort. There are too many negatives associated with punishment to use it casually. When an effective punishment can be found, one that is more powerful than the competing reinforcement yet not threatening enough to bring out a fear response, this technique can work very effectively.

Counter-conditioning. Counter-conditioning is the most effective of the three extinction techniques we list and we have put it off until last because it is the most complex and because the withdrawal of reinforcement is generally effective in nine out of ten instances. Counter-conditioning can be administered in many ways but the most common way is to set up two competing responses and reinforce one but *not* reinforce the other. The way this works is to do the analysis of the behavior you want to extinguish, identify the reinforcer controlling that behavior and then identify another behavior that could occur instead of the inappropriate behavior but could not occur at the same time as the inappropriate behavior. Then you shape the new behavior and use the reinforcers you have identified for the inappropriate behavior as the reinforcers for the new behavior—while absolutely withholding reinforcement for the inappropriate behavior. What you are doing is reinforcing the horse for doing what *you* want it to do and not reinforcing the horse for what *it* wants to do. Another way to say this is that the horse wants something (the reinforcers) and you want something (an appropriate behavior). You are going to give the horse what it wants for doing what you want.

An example of this procedure will probably be the best way for you to see how you might apply counter-conditioning. Let us assume that Ben, an old quarter horse, has picked up the bad habit (from his owner's point of view) of shaking his head from side to side when the owner is mounted on him and at a standstill. Why does this behavior occur? Well, the only way to determine this is to observe the behavior several times and try to see what the consequences of the behavior are. As we observe, we notice that the rider unconsciously pets Ben on the neck and says soothing things to him with great regularity after the head-shaking behavior. We don't know absolutely, but we can assume that this is the consequence maintaining the behavior. Ben merely wants a little bit of additional attention and has found a way to get it.

Now that we have made a tentative identification of the reinforcers maintaining the behavior, let's identify an incompatible, competing behavior that cannot occur at the same time as head-shaking. How about holding-the-head-still behavior? A horse cannot shake its head and hold its head still at the same time. The two behaviors are incompatible; they compete. Now let's withdraw the reinforcer for the inappropriate behavior and provide the reinforcer only for the competing behavior we have chosen. In other words, no more petting and talking for head-shaking. These reinforcers will now be given to Ben only when we catch him holding his head still. Ben, wanting the reinforcer, and not being stupid, will soon catch on and if our rider is consistent, will soon be rid of an irritating behavior. The idea is to catch the horse being good and provide it with the reinforcer then and only then.

SUMMARY

In this chapter we outlined the basic principles of operant psychology. As horse trainers, we are in the business of causing learning to occur, and since learning itself cannot be directly observed, we must base our training procedures on the *effects* we have on behavior. If behavior changes, we infer that learning has occurred.

Learning is governed by the interaction of an organism with the environment. The environment is composed of five kinds of stimuli, each of which has a different kind of effect on organisms. We may use reinforcing stimuli to shape new behaviors, a process which is the step-by-step training of a new behavior through reinforcing successive approximations of the new behavior. Behaviors then appear in different situations because of a generalization process and organisms learn to restrict some behaviors to specific situations through discrimination. The best way to teach a new behavior is by using a one-for-one schedule of reinforcement, and this schedule may then be stretched by gradually leaving out some reinforcers. Some behaviors are maintained via internalized reinforcement.

Extinction, the unlearning of behaviors, can be brought about in three ways: through the removal of reinforcement, the replacement of reinforcement with punishment and through counter-conditioning. The process of unlearning a behavior is pretty much the same as teaching a new one in the first place. The keys to teaching and extinguishing behaviors are observation and consistency.

The topics in this chapter, while fairly technical, give you the basic knowledge to modify any equine behavior and, indeed, the behavior of any organism. The last chapter of this book draws heavily on the concepts outlined in this chapter. Specific training techniques are built directly upon operant theory.

CHAPTER 7

Animal Psychopathology

We have presented a number of relatively simple reinforcement procedures that can be used to train a horse to behave in a number of ways. These techniques are easy to use, and the reader really doesn't have to learn a great deal of psychological theory to understand how they work. There are times, however, when the horse owner will be faced with complex behavioral problems that are not easily modified through the application of reinforcement procedures. These types of problems usually occur when high levels of anxiety and fear are present in the horse, and when depression may also be an occasional problem. While terms like neurotic and depression are usually reserved for human beings, they are also descriptive of emotional disorders in animals.

In the previous chapter, we focused upon the horse's overt behavior. In this chapter, we are going to be concentrating upon the emotional state of your animal, and we will attempt to specify those conditions that lead to the development of undesirable emotional states. By undesirable, we mean emotional states that make it difficult for your horse to get along with people and to perform tasks efficiently. Just as it is difficult for an anxious person to work efficiently at his or her job, it is also difficult for an anxious horse to perform tasks as efficiently as it could were it more relaxed. Frequently, an anxious or depressed horse is simply written off. In these cases, behavioral problems are usually attributed to bad breeding or stupidity on the part of the animal. This is very unfortunate for the simple reason that those internal states that are disrupting the animal's behavior can, under many circumstances, be changed. In this chapter we will discuss techniques to alleviate these problems and we will look more closely at anxiety and depression as it may occur in your horse.

ANXIETY AND AVERSIVE EVENTS

In a previous chapter, we defined punishment as a stimulus that when applied after a behavior causes the behavior to decrease or to be totally eliminated. There are many different theories that explain the effects of punishment in different ways, but most would agree that a punishing or noxious stimulus is one that elicits fear from an organism. If an animal is punished for a specific behavior, all it has to do to avoid fear is to stop engaging in that behavior. Ideally, that is exactly what happens. The fear, in fact, motivates the animal to stop misbehaving. Unfortunately, in real life, things do not work that simply. As your horse matures, it will experience many aversive events that are not under its control or the control of the owner. Occasionally, the horse may detect fear-producing stimuli of which the owner is totally unaware. Perhaps the horse senses that other horses are afraid and it responds by also becoming fearful. Often, through complex conditioning processes, relatively neutral events begin to signal danger to your horse. The horse responds by becoming afraid. It is these fearful states that make animals highly anxious and neurotic, and the formation of these emotional states usually is closely related to some punishing or aversive event that the animal has experienced in the past.

In order to understand how these complex psychological processes work, the reader must develop some understanding of how punishment works. We will try to identify those variables that determine exactly what kind of effect an aversive event will have upon your horse. Unfortunately, this is not a simple matter. As one prominent researcher in the area has remarked ". . . considerable uncertainty remains today regarding the effect of punishment, and there does not appear to be any single reliable effect" (Church, 1963). As discouraging as this statement may seem, the reader should be able to develop a good understanding of how aversive events often serve to make animals neurotic. A thorough understanding of the effects of punishment will also enable the horse owner to use punishment as a behavior change technique.

Parameters of Punishment

There are a number of variables that interact to determine how an aversive or punishing event will affect an animal. One of the most important variables is the intensity of the aversive event. The principle has been demonstrated in numerous experiments in which an animal is punished (usually with an electric shock) for emitting a certain behavior (e.g., Azrin, Holz, & Hake, 1963). The experimenter divides the animals into different groups and proceeds to apply a different intensity of punishment to each group. Once the behavior has been punished, it occurs less frequently. It has been found that the degree of behavioral suppression produced by the punishment is a directly increasing function of the intensity of punishment (Karsh, 1962). An intensely averse event may merely serve to keep the animal on edge without suppressing behavior to a significant degree. Mild punishment may also serve as a signal to the animal that something is amiss.

What does this mean to the horse owner? If you are using punishment as a technique to suppress a behavior, you need to apply punishment of a sufficient intensity. We firmly believe, however, that punishment should be used only when absolutely necessary. Reinforcement techniques are much more effective because they do not produce anxiety in the animal. All the animal owner needs to do is to reinforce a behavior that is incompatible with the undesired behavior.

Another important variable that determines the effect a punishing stimulus will have on an animal is time. Experimental evidence has shown that punishment is most effective when it is administered right after a behavior has occurred (Azrin, 1956; Skinner, 1938). A good example of this rule is presented in an experiment that tested the effects of delayed punishment on dogs (Solomon, Turner, & Lessac, 1968). The experimenters were studying the behavioral effects of different delays of punishment on a training plan designed to teach dogs to resist the temptation to eat food from a plate. During the training phase two bowls of food were placed in front of each animal. One contained dry food and the other contained horsemeat. The animals were allowed to eat the dry food, but were hit across the snout for eating the horsemeat. The dogs were divided into three experimental groups and each group was punished in a slightly different manner. The animals in the first group (zero second-delay group) were punished as soon as they touched the horsemeat, while another group (5 second-delay group) was punished 5 seconds after eating the horsemeat. The animals in the third group (15 second-delay group) were swatted with the newspaper 15 seconds after eating the horsemeat. The animals were never punished for eating the dry food. All of the dogs were trained in this manner until they had gone 20 consecutive days without touching the horsemeat. The experimenter then wanted to see how long each group would continue to resist the temptation to eat the horsemeat, even though punishment was no longer being applied. Even though the three groups of dogs learned to avoid the horsemeat in the same period of time, they were much different in terms of how long they avoided the temptation of eating the horsemeat again. The animals that had been punished as soon as they touched the meat resisted temptation for much longer than the other two groups. The time interval between eating the horsemeat and the application of punishment was inversely related to resistance to temptation.

These findings contain important implications for the horse owner. If an aversive stimulus is to be used during training, it should be applied either as the undesirable behavior occurs or *immediately* afterwards. When these conditions are not met, punishment will not only be ineffective, it will also serve to make the animal highly anxious and confused. Any animal that experiences aversive events not closely associated with a specific behavior may well develop a neurotic condition. We will discuss this phenomenon more fully later in this chapter.

There is another important variable that must be taken into account when attempting to predict the effect of an aversive event. One must ascertain the manner in which the behavior to be punished was originally learned. When punishment immediately follows a behavior that was learned through the use of positive rewards, the probability of that behavior recurring is quite low. But what if that behavior had been learned through the application of punishment techniques? Behaviors that have been learned through the use of punishment are called avoidance behaviors, and they are reinforced by the absence of punishment. Therefore, if you punish these behaviors, they will increase instead of decreasing! Obviously, it is very important to determine how a behavior was learned before you punish it.

We have seen that an aversive event may have two different effects on an animal. When it is under the control of an individual who understands how punishment works, it may be an effective behavior-change technique. Punishment should only be used when it will be effective after a few administrations. It should also only be used when some alternative behavior is available to the animal. It has been demonstrated that punishment is effective when alternative behaviors are simultaneously reinforced, but when punishment is administered by itself and no alternative behaviors are available it is often ineffective (Sears, Macoby, & Levin, 1957). Along similar lines, a prominent researcher in the field has stated that punishment is only effective ". . . as an aid to the reinforcement of new responses" (Solomon, 1964).

By gaining an understanding of how aversive events may be used to effectively condition good behaviors, we may also begin to see how aversive events might lead to the formation of highly undesirable emotional states. When an animal experiences punishment in a situation where there's no alternative behavior or much time has elapsed between the behavior and the punishment, the animal may become neurotic. This may happen in a variety of different ways. Perhaps the owner is impatient and does not use punishment correctly. In some cases, the horse may experience aversive events that are not under the control of the owner. The result, in both cases, is a traumatized animal.

Conditioning Emotional States

We have stated that aversive events may make a horse susceptible to anxiety and neurotic conditions. In order to understand how this happens one must become familiar with a phenomenon called a conditioned emotional response. The average horse owner has probably observed signs of fear or anxiety in their horse when there was no apparent reason for the animal to be afraid. If one carefully analyzes these situations, however, one will discover that there are certain stimuli in the evironment that are triggering the anxiety or, as we shall call it, the conditioned emotional response. Why does an apparently neutral stimulus elicit fear from your horse? It is because that neutral stimulus has been previously paired or associated with an aversive event in such a way that the horse now regards the neutral stimulus as a signal that something bad is going to happen. Thus, the horse becomes fearful.

The reader may remember from our chapter on conditioning that when an unconditioned stimulus (US), such as an electric shock or the smell of meat, is repeatedly paired with a neutral or conditioned stimulus (CS) such as a light or bell, the previously neutral stimulus begins to elicit the same response that the unconditioned stimulus elicited. You can perform a simple experiment with your horse to demonstrate this phenomenon. Simply sound a buzzer (CS) and, at the same time, give the horse something good to eat (US). Repeat the procedure ten or fifteen times. Now try sounding the buzzer without giving the horse its favorite snack. The horse should salivate in response to the buzzer. An observer who did not know about the conditioning that had taken place might wonder what is wrong with your horse. After all, there is nothing appetizing about a buzzer. The answer, of course, is that the observer is witnessing a conditioned response to a neutral stimulus. When the conditioned response is not something concrete like salivation, but is an emotional reaction (e.g., fear), then we say that we have witnessed a conditioned emotional response (CER).

When will a conditioned emotional response (CER) be learned? Solomon and Wynne (1954) have found that there are three conditions which must be met for a CER to become associated with a previously neutral stimulus. First, the aversive stimulus must be strong enough to elicit a pain-fear reaction. Second, the aversive stimulus must occur at pretty much the same time as the conditioned (previously neutral) stimulus. That is, there should be reasonable temporal contiguity. Third, the pairing of the two stimuli must be repeated a number of times. If these three conditions are met, a conditioned emotional response will be learned.

If your horse should learn to become anxious in the presence of a particular stimulus, it is quite possible that that emotional response will generalize to other stimuli. Miller (1935) performed an experiment which provides a good example of how this type of generalization occurs. In his study, rats were shocked every time they approached a small cup from which they had previously been trained to drink. The rats, of course, learned to become afraid of the food cup (CER). But, they also learned to become anxious in the presence of other objects that looked like the food cup. The anxiety had generalized to other stimuli. This is one of the problems to be dealt with when trying to detect what stimulus is making a horse anxious. The stimulus that is eliciting the anxiety may not be one that was previously paired with an aversive event. It may merely be similar to the stimulus that was originally paired with punishment. This makes detection of the conditioned stimuli a difficult matter. We will explain how these stimuli may be identified in a later section.

Anxiety and Conflict

One of the crucial factors usually involved in the development of behavior disorders is conflict. Conflict may be defined as a psychological state produced by the competition between several incompatible responses. If one wants to do two completely different things at the same time a state of conflict is produced. Conflict is usually characterized by the presence of tension, anxiety and fearfulness.

In order to better understand the dynamics of conflict, it might be advantageous to look at the experimental paradigm typically used to study conflicted states. Usually a rat is placed in an apparatus consisting of two small chambers joined by a narrow runway. The rat is placed in the runway and it is trained to run to one of the chambers. In our example, this chamber would be painted white so that the rat could easily distinguish it from the other chamber, which is painted black. If the animal runs into the black chamber, it receives a painful electric shock. Soon, the animal learns to avoid the black chamber and it quickly runs into the white chamber. In order to demonstrate the presence of conflict, the experimenter could play a nasty trick on the poor rat. All the experimenter does is paint both of the chambers black and place the rat in the runway. When this is done, the rat doesn't know where to go because it associates both of the chambers with punishment. That is, it has learned a conditioned emotional response (CER) to both chambers. Typically, the rat will stay in the middle of the runway and cower as it tries to figure out a solution to its dilemma. This type of conflict has been called an avoidance-avoidance conflict (Miller, 1971) because both of the alternatives available to the animal are ones that it would like to avoid. One might say that the animal must choose the lesser of two evils. But this is not the only type of conflict. What if we had painted both of the chambers white? Although this would have a less traumatic situation for the rat, it still would have produced a state of conflict in that the animal wouldn't know to which chamber it should run. When this experiment is performed, the rat usually spends a period of time in the runway nervously looking toward each of the chambers. Finally, it will resolve the conflict and run to one of the chambers. This is called an approach-approach conflict, because the animal must choose between two incompatible responses, each of which has been rewarded in the past.

The type of conflict that the horse owner is most likely to encounter is an approach-avoidance conflict, and it occurs when an animal wants to approach and avoid the same object. This type of conflict is usually studied by placing a rat in an apparatus which consists of a long runway with a chamber on one end. The chamber contains a food dispenser, and the rat is trained to run the length of the runway to receive food from the dispenser. After the rat has mastered the task, it is put in the runway and just as it approaches the chamber it receives an electric shock. This procedure is repeated several times and soon the hungry rat has two conflicting desires. It wants to run to the chamber so that it can eat. But, it also wants to avoid the chamber so that it won't get shocked. Typically, the animal will run up the runway until it is about a foot from the chamber, and then it will stop and retreat to a safer position. This behavior pattern will be repeated for hours as the animal alternates between approaching and avoiding the chamber.

If this behavior seems peculiar, you might look at your own behavior. Approach-avoidance conflicts are common in human beings. Take the case of the passive young employee who, at the urging of her mate, decides to ask her employer for a raise, only to chicken out at the last minute. Surely the reader has, at one time or another, had to do something that he or she was afraid to do. If you think back, you will remember that your anxiety increased as you got closer to the point of having to perform the unpleasant task. Similarly, you probably felt less anxious if you stepped back and got some distance from the unpleasant task which made you so nervous. You were caught in an approach-avoidance conflict and, like the rat, your anxiety increased as you approached the goal and it decreased when you avoided it. The primary characteristic of these conflicts is that the urge to approach the goal is strongest when the animal is furthest away from the goal. As the animal gets closer to the goal the urge to approach decreases and the desire to avoid increases. The desire to avoid is strongest when the animal is closest to the goal. There is a point at which the desire to approach is just as strong as the desire to avoid. It is at this point that the animal tends to really vacillate between the desire to approach and to avoid. The poor animal is caught in an inescapable dilemma and, much like the human neurotic, it will vacillate between approach behavior and avoidance behavior and will ultimately become quite neurotic.

To a certain extent, conflicts of this nature are a part of life and are unavoidable. They can be minimized if the animal owner is aware of how these conflicts are learned. It is important that they be minimized, because they generate anxiety and if they are severe enough they may lead to neurotic conditions. As we have shown, the horse will develop this type of conflict if it is punished and rewarded for engaging in the same behavior. If the horse owner is consistent in the manner in which he or she rewards and punishes behaviors, the probability of these conflicts occurring will be minimized. Similarly, the horse owner should ensure that the horse is not traumatized while engaging in behaviors that will be rewarded at a later time. A race horse, for example, should not be exposed to aversive circumstances while at a race track. No matter how much the horse loves to run, aversive events will make it somewhat conflicted about performing in the presence of stimuli which are anxiety producing. Conflict and anxiety, when severe, do disrupt performance, and the horse will not run as fast as it is capable of running.

Experimental Neurosis

We have used the term neurotic quite frequently in this chapter. Exactly what is a neurosis? A leading researcher in the area, D.O. Hebb (1947), has defined neurosis as "... an undesirable emotional condition which is generalized and persistent." There are actually many ways of defining neurosis. We will define it as an emotional state characterized by a high degree of anxiety which seems to disrupt much of the behavior of the organism.

Psychologists have long been concerned with developing techniques to cure or alleviate neurotic conditions. Because a large segment of the human population suffers from neurotic conditions, much research effort has been expended in this direction. One strategy researchers use is to make animals neurotic and then try to find a technique to cure that same neurotic condition. The general idea is that if you can cure neurotic animals you can also cure neurotic people. Although this is a highly questionable assumption, these studies are valuable to us because they should help us to identify those variables that play a role in the development of undesirable behavioral conditions.

Traditionally, two different methods have been used to produce experimental neuroses in animals. In one, the experimenter attempts to evoke two incompatible responses at the same time. This produces a state of conflict. The second procedure involves the repeated application of an aversive stimulus. Simply put, the animal is punished on so many occasions that it becomes neurotic.

Pavlov (1927), the Nobel Prize winning Russian physiologist, was the first to induce an experimental neurosis in animals. In his experiments, dogs were trained to salivate whenever a circle lit up in their experimental chamber. They did this by pairing the circle with the presentation of food. Soon, the circle began to automatically elicit a salivation response. At other times, an ellipse would light up in the chamber. When the ellipse lit up, no food was given to the dog. This training procedure produced a dog that would eagerly salivate when a circle would light up, but would sit quietly in a corner when the ellipse lit up. Each shape took on an entirely different meaning to the animal. But then Pavlov began to gradually change the shape of the ellipse, in such a way that it became difficult for the dog to tell the difference between the two signals. Soon the dogs became confused and the same stimulus began to elicit two different responses. As we have explained, when an animal feels a need to emit two different responses at the same time, a state of conflict is produced. The animals in Pavlov's experiment became so anxious that whenever they were placed in the chamber their behavioral functioning would become disrupted. They would usually sit passively in the corner of the chamber and shake uncontrollably.

This type of experiment led Pavlov to speculate that there are two basic processes present in the nervous system: excitation processes and inhibition processes. He believed that under certain conditions these processes would become overloaded, and that the animal would become neurotic. This overloading of the nervous system would occur when the animal was faced with a task that produced a great deal of strain or stress. In some situations, for example, the animal would want to respond in a given manner but would feel that it should inhibit itself. A state of conflict would be produced and much strain would be placed on the animal's inhibitory processes. Finally, the conflict would be too much for the animal to tolerate, and the inhibitory mechanisms would overload, causing a neurotic condition. In other situations, the excitatory processes would become overloaded. This would happen when the animal is repeatedly subjected to excessive stimulation (e.g., punishment). We see then that there would be two types of neuroses. An animal with inhibitory overload would be more depressed, fearful and inhibited, while animals suffering from excitatory overload would be restless, aggressive and unrestrained (Kurstin, 1968).

Those circumstances that would result in excitatory overload have much in common with those methods used by another group of psychologists to produce neurotic conditions in animals. In these studies an aversive stimulus is repeatedly applied to an animal that cannot escape or avoid the stimuli's punishing effects. In one of these experiments,

Masserman and Pechtel (1953) attempted to produce a neurosis in monkeys. The monkeys were first trained to perform a relatively complicated task for which they received a reward. After they had learned to perform this task, the animals were exposed to a threatening experience. The threatening experience was repeated numerous times and it consisted of an experimenter waving a toy snake in front of the monkey. (As strange as it may seem, this procedure had been previously demonstrated to be extremely traumatic to monkeys.) In this particular experiment, the procedure produced an animal which suffered from generalized inhibitions, phobias, compulsions, severe somatic disturbances, neuromuscular disabilities, sexual deviations and abnormal social behavior. Obviously, the presence of the toy snakes completely traumatized the monkey. When the procedure was performed, the monkeys would not attack the snakes but would run about their cage, terrified. Several monkeys even appeared to be hallucinating.

Obviously, the monkeys in Masserman's experiment were extremely neurotic. There has been some debate, however, concerning that part of the procedure that made them neurotic. Was it the repeated punishments alone or was a state of conflict produced in the monkeys? Because they were working for a food reward just before they were shown the snake, it is possible that they learned an approach-avoidance conflict (i.e., approach the food but avoid the snake). Some experts argue that a state of conflict must be created if a neurotic condition is to be produced. Others argue that the repeated application of an aversive stimulus will produce a neurosis, regardless of whether a conflict is present in the animal. The data, in our opinion, would seem to indicate that while a prolonged state of conflict will produce a neurosis, repeated punishment alone will also create the same effect. The wise horse owner will do everything in his or her power to insure that the horse is not exposed to either type of treatment.

Depression

The reader will remember that punishment is most effective when it immediately follows the behavior one wants to eliminate. One of the primary reasons for this is for the animal to know what behavior is being punished. This means that it has some control over the aversive events which it is experiencing. There are times, however, when an animal experiences an aversive event over which it has no control. This may happen to a horse whose owner punishes it indiscriminately, or it may occur when an animal's environment contains an aversive feature or component which the animal cannot escape or avoid. The consequences of these types of events have been graphically demonstrated in a series of experiments by Martin Seligman (1968). Seligman would strap animals into a hammock that made it impossible for the animal to move. The animals were then administered sixty-four moderately painful electric shocks on a random basis so that the animals had no idea when the shocks would occur. The next day these animals (in this case dogs) were trained to perform a task which dogs normally are capable of learning in a very few moments. This task required them to jump over a barrier in order to avoid an electric shock. But Seligman's dogs behaved in a peculiar manner. Instead of trying to jump over the barrier, they would passively sit in the corner of the apparatus and endure the shock.

The behavior of the dogs was not restricted to the apparatus in which they were originally shocked. It was reported that the animals acted as if they were in their home cages. While normal dogs would bark at visitors, these helpless dogs would practically roll over on their backs with their tails between their legs. Observations revealed that they became extremely passive in any situation which called for any type of active coping behavior.

The question became one of identifying that part of the experimental treatment that led to the learning of this passive behavior. Was it the fact that the animals had no control over the shock or was it simply the result of receiving a lot of punishment? This question has been answered through the use of what is called a yoked control group. In this type of experiment, one group of animals (Group A) is placed in the hammocks, just as they were in the first experiment. These animals can, however, turn off the shock by touching a button with their noses. In the chambers next door to these animals there are other animals (Group B) strapped into similar hammocks. The shocking devices hooked up to the animals in Group A are fixed in such a way that they trigger the shocking devices worn by the animals in Group B. Whenever an animal in Group A gets a shock, the corresponding animal in Group B gets one also. When the animal in Group A hits its nose on the button, it automatically turns off the shock it is receiving and also terminates the shock that the animal in Group B is receiving. In this way, the animals in each group receive the same amount of shock in exactly the same sequences. The only difference is that the animals in Group A can cope with the situation by turning off the shock, while the animals in Group B receive the same amount of shock but have no control over any aspect of its administration. As it turned out, the animals that could turn off the shock (Group A) did not become helpless, while the other animals developed the same behavior described in Seligman's first experiment. Seligman has labeled this phenomenon learned helplessness.

The establishment of learned helplessness is apparently due to the fact that the animal cannot control the trauma it is experiencing. The frequency, intensity, duration and timing of the shock make little difference (Seligman, 1975) and this phenomenon has been established in many species. Seligman believes that the behavior of these animals is analogous to a state of depression in humans. Many behavioral psychologists believe that humans become depressed when the same type of situation is encountered. That is, when humans have no control over the consequences of their own behavior they too will learn to become helpless and depressed. Interestingly enough, there is also data to indicate that animals will develop learned helplessness when they have no control over the rewards they receive.

ANXIETY REDUCTION TECHNIQUES

We have discussed the manner in which animals may become highly anxious and neurotic. If the horse owner understands how anxiety is produced in animals, he or she may be able to prevent the formation of neurotic disorders in his or her horse. There may be times, however, when the horse owner will be confronted with a neurotic animal that must be treated. In this section, we will present those techniques that have been used to reduce anxiety in both humans and animals. Although these methods have been proven to be quite effective, they are not that easy to implement.

We have explained that animals develop anxiety as a result of some sort of traumatic or aversive experience. When the animal initially experiences this aversive event, it associates the fear with some external stimulus. Those stimuli that were originally paired with the aversive events are called the primary stimuli. As time passes, the anxiety or fear which the horse experiences around the primary stimuli begins to spread or generalize to other stimuli. These stimuli usually resemble the primary stimuli in some way and they may be called secondary stimuli. If, for example, a person is in a car accident, it is quite possible that they will develop an anxiety response to automobiles. The primary stimulus which was originally associated with the trauma is an automobile. Whenever this individual is inside of a car, he or she may become afraid. But the anxiety may generalize to other stimuli. The sound of a horn, the sight of a highway or the thought of travel may make the person very anxious. These stimuli are the secondary stimuli.

This spreading of anxiety has been called primary stimulus generalization, and it accounts for the manner in which neurotic behavior seems to spread from one situation to another. Despite the fact that the anxiety was originally associated with one specific stimulus, primary stimulus generalization often serves to produce an emotional state that does not appear to be in response to anything in the environment. If one carefully examines the situation, however, it will become apparent that the animal's anxiety is in response to external stimuli. The anxiety reaches its greatest intensity when the animal is exposed to the original primary stimuli, and the anxiety decreases as the similarity between the primary and the secondary stimuli decreases. If your horse is neurotic you should be able to identify the primary stimuli by systematically assessing the intensity of the horse's anxiety in different situations. When you have identified that specific stimulus that elicits the most intense anxiety in your horse, you can be sure that you have identified the primary stimulus determinant of the animal's neurotic behavior. Because this identification process can be quite complicated, we will discuss it in greater detail.

Identification of Primary Stimulus Determinants

In order to identify the primary stimulus determinants of an animal's anxiety, one must carefully observe and record the animal's behavior. First, the horse owner should determine those conditions under which the animal is not anxious. On a sheet of paper, record all of those stimuli that are present when the horse is in a relaxed state. Then begin to record those times and places in which the animal appears to be anxious. It is important that two other pieces of information be recorded: (1) all of those stimuli present must be identified and (2) the intensity of the horse's anxiety must be estimated. The best way to record the animal's anxiety level is to use a one to ten scale in which ten represents the highest level of anxiety you have ever witnessed in your animal and, a designation of one indicates that the animal is completely relaxed and absolutely no anxiety is present. It is imperative that you carefully record all of this data for a two or three week period. Even though this is a boring task, the success of the treatment is dependent upon accurate data collection. Once you have identified a number of situations in which your horse becomes anxious, you may attempt to identify those stimuli that are present in all of those situations. In other words, there should be specific stimuli that are present when your horse is most anxious. Perhaps the animal experiences high levels of anxiety in certain places or after it has been asked to perform certain tasks. The possibilities are endless, but the horse owner should be able to identify a set of stimulus conditions that are present whenever the animal is highly anxious. Those stimuli are the primary stimulus determinants of the anxiety, and they are the stimuli which you will focus upon during the treatment phase.

Anxiety Reduction

When anxiety is viewed as an emotional response that has been associated with certain stimuli through a conditioning process, it becomes clear that that emotional response can be deconditioned. Wolpe (1966) has investigated the nature of anxiety, and he has noted that anxiety may be viewed in terms of how it operates physiologically. Anxiety, he explains, is mediated through the autonomic nervous system. This autonomic nervous system consists of two different parts: the sympathetic nervous system and the parasympathetic nervous system. When an animal is anxious its sympathetic nervous system immediately becomes activated. Conversely, when an animal is in a relaxed state its parasympathetic nervous system is operational. Thus, one might say that the sympathetic system mediates anxiety and the parasympathetic system mediates relaxation. But we are leaving out a very important aspect about this autonomic nervous system. The two systems (sympathetic and parasympathetic) are antagonistic to one another. This means that when one turns on, the other one automatically turns off.

What are the implications of the fact that these two systems are antagonistic? It occurred to Wolpe that if you could somehow get an animal's parasympathetic system to turn on under those conditions in which the animal usually gets anxious, that the animal would relax. This would happen because when the parasympathetic system is operating, the sympathetic system (which mediates anxiety) must turn off. If this occurred a number of times, the animal's anxiety response to certain stimuli might become deconditioned. That is, the animal would learn to relax.

How does one manipulate an animal in such a way that its parasympathetic system becomes operational? Wolpe noted that there are certain activities that are incompatible with anxiety and are mediated by the parasympathetic system. Sex, for example, is incompatible with anxiety to the extent that the male is unable to achieve an erection when anxious (sex is incompatible with the operation of the sympathetic system). A state of deep relaxation is also incompatible with anxiety. There is a problem, however. Responses of these types (sex, relaxation, etc.) will serve to inhibit anxiety only if they are of greater intensity than the anxiety response. If the anxiety response is more intense than the state of relaxation, then it is the state of relaxation which will be inhibited. What Wolpe proposed to do was to pair a parasympathetic activity (relaxation) with an anxiety-producing stimulus that only elicited very low levels of anxiety. We previously identified these types of stimuli as secondary stimuli. That is, they are similar enough to the primary stimulus determinant to cause the animal to become afraid, but the animal does not become as afraid as it would if the primary stimulus itself were present. If the anxiety response to the secondary stimuli is weak enough, an activity mediated by the parasympathetic system should be able to override it. Soon the animal learns that it can be relaxed in the presence of a stimulus which used to make it mildly anxious. The anxiety has been deconditioned. Now the animal trainer can do the same thing with a secondary stimulus that is slightly more similar to the primary stimulus and accomplish the same result. By repeating this procedure with secondary stimuli that become increasingly similar to the primary stimulus, one can ultimately decondition the anxiety response to the primary stimulus determinant itself.

Perhaps it would be helpful to give a concrete example of how this procedure has been implemented. In one of his early experiments, Wolpe (1952) used one of the counterconditioning procedures to eliminate the fear which his cats had learned to experience whenever a buzzer was sounded. Whenever the buzzer was sounded Wolpe's cats would become incredibly anxious and would urinate and shake uncontrollably. First Wolpe had to find an activity that was mediated by the parasympathetic system and that inhibited anxiety. He decided to use eating behavior because it had been previously demonstrated to have a soothing effect that counteracted anxiety (Masserman, 1943). Because high levels of anxiety would inhibit eating, he initially paired the eating behavior with an extremely low level of anxiety. Wolpe did this by placing his cats forty feet away from the buzzer, so that the cats could barely hear the sound and would not get very anxious. After the animals had eaten a little bit of food, their anxiety decreased and they actually seemed to relax. At that point, Wolpe would move them a little bit closer to the buzzer and feed them again. Once again, the animals experienced only a low level of anxiety and this anxiety was soon inhibited as the animals relaxed and ate the food. By gradually moving the animals closer and closer to the buzzer (over a period of several days) and repeatedly pairing the buzzer with a relaxed state, the animal's anxiety was eliminated. A number of cats that had appeared to be quite neurotic now behaved in a completely normal fashion.

Wolpe calls this type of procedure "psychotherapy by reciprocal inhibition" but it is usually referred to as systematic desensitization. Although many have questioned the validity of Wolpe's theories, no one doubts that the technique actually does work. Numerous investigators utilizing animals as experimental subjects have found that these procedures may be used to eliminate anxiety (Gordon and Bacon, 1971; Reid, Hunsicker, Sautter and Miller, 1972; Hunsicker, Nelson and Reid, 1973) and the technique also works with people. Wolpe (1958) reported that in one experiment 210 patients received this treatment and the success rate was a staggering 89.5 percent. Lazarus (1971) reported a cure rate of 78 percent and other experimenters have also stated that the technique is very effective (Lang and Lazovik, 1963; Paul, 1966, 1969).

Clinical Application of Systematic Desensitization

There are three factors that are extremely important when attempting to decondition anxiety through the use of systematic desensitization. First, the trainer must select an anxiety-inhibiting stimulus that is strong enough to countercondition the anxiety-eliciting stimuli. As we have already stated, eating is an effective counterconditioning agent. Any treatment that will relax your animal should be helpful. If the horse owner possesses a horse that is easily calmed through petting and verbal reassurance, relaxation may well be the best counterconditioner. Another critical factor is that the anxiety-inhibiting stimuli must be initially paired with very low levels of anxiety. Animal owners who are unsuccessful when using this technique usually fail because they initially attempt to countercondition too high a level of anxiety. Remember, begin by attempting to induce a relaxed state when the animal is experiencing an extremely low level of anxiety. The third critical factor is that the anxiety-inhibiting stimuli must be paired contiguously with the anxiety-eliciting stimuli. The aversive stimulus will not lose its anxiety arousing properties if it is not simultaneously paired with the anxiety-inhibiting stimuli.

It might be advantageous to construct a sample treatment plan. Our patient is a horse that is often used by its owner to go hunting. The horse owner conscientiously keeps behavioral records and discovers that his horse becomes slightly anxious whenever it sees that a gun is present. When the horse is saddled and ridden on an actual hunt, the horse's anxiety increases and when the gun is fired the horse becomes very afraid. This anxiety has generalized to the point where it is slightly anxious whenever the hunter takes it for a ride. The owner has, however, been very astute and he has noticed that when the horse is ridden by his son (who has never taken the horse hunting) it is completely relaxed. By examining his records, the horse owner has determined that the horse experiences the highest level of anxiety when the gun is fired. This means that the firing of the gun is the primary stimulus determinant. He then ranks the other activities that make the horse anxious according to the amount of anxiety each activity produces. The result is a list of events in which the event at the top of the list elicits the most anxiety (e.g., gun firing) and the event at the bottom of the list elicits the least anxiety (e.g., hunter, unarmed, saddles the horse). This list is called a stimulus hierarchy, and the stimuli should be ordered in such a way that each event or stimulus presentation elicits more anxiety than did the previous stimulus presentation. That is, each event has a slightly higher potential for eliciting anxiety than the previous one on the list.

The horse owner must then select an anxiety-inhibiting agent. In this case we shall use sugar cubes because the horse has previously demonstrated a preference for them. The actual treatment will involve three phases: (1) desensitizing the horse to the hunter, (2) desensitizing the horse to the sight of the gun and (3) desensitizing the horse to the sound of gun firing. The important thing to remember in organizing the hierarchy is that the initial exposure should elicit very low levels of anxiety and that the subsequent presentations should be graduated so that the anxiety experienced by the horse at any one time is always minimal. In this particular case, the initial exposure involves the unarmed hunter taking the horse out of the barn for a short walk. This should not elicit much anxiety from the horse, and if it does the horse owner should immediately return the horse to the barn. The horse owner must be patient. It is better to be cautious than to ruin the entire procedure by exposing the animal to too intense a level of anxiety. The following is a sample of hierarchy for this type of treatment plan.

STEP 1:   Trainer (unarmed) takes horse out of barn for
                one minute. The entire time, the animal is
                being soothed and fed sugar cubes.

STEP 2:   Trainer (unarmed) takes horse out of barn for
                two minutes. The entire time, the animal is
                being soothed and fed sugar cubes.

STEP 3:   Trainer (unarmed) takes horse out of barn for
               three minutes. The entire time, the animal is
               being soothed and fed sugar cubes.

STEP 4:   Trainer (unarmed) takes horse out of barn for
               four minutes. The entire time, the animal is
               being soothed and fed sugar cubes.

STEP 5:   Trainer (unarmed) takes horse out of barn for
               five minutes. The entire time, the animal is
               being soothed and fed sugar cubes.

STEP 6:   Trainer (unarmed) takes horse out of barn for
               ten minutes. The entire time, the animal is
               being soothed and fed sugar cubes.

STEP 7:   Trainer (unarmed) takes horse out of barn for
               fifteen minutes. The entire time, the animal
               is being soothed and fed sugar cubes.

Note that one does not advance to the next step until the
horse is *completely comfortable* with the preceding step. This
means that any one of the steps may have to be repeated a
number of times. When all seven steps of the first phase
have been completed, the animal should be completely desensitized to the hunter. Now the horse must be desensitized
to the gun! This could be accomplished by using the steps
outlined below. Remember, if the animal becomes highly
anxious it should be returned to the barn immediately. The
next day, it should be returned *to the previous step* in the
hierarchy.

STEP 8:   The trainer takes the horse out for a one
                 minute walk. The gun is leaning against a
                 fence where it can be seen by the horse. The
                 animal is soothed and fed continuously.

STEP 9:   The trainer takes the horse out for a two
                 minute walk. The gun is leaning against a
                 fence where it can be seen by the horse. The
                 animal is soothed and fed continuously.

STEP 10:   The trainer takes the horse out for a three
                 minute walk. The gun is leaning against a
                 fence where it can be seen by the horse. The
                 animal is soothed and fed continuously.

STEPS 11 through 15: The horse is taken for walks in the
                 same manner as STEPS 8 through 10. Each
                 time, however, the horse is walked closer to
                 the gun.

STEP 16:   The horse is walked over to the gun and the
                 trainer stops the horse and keeps it in that
                 location for one minute. The horse is soothed
                 and fed.

STEP 17:   The horse is walked over to the gun and the
                 trainer stops the horse and keeps it in that
                 location for two minutes. The horse is
                 soothed and fed.

STEP 18:   The horse is walked over to the gun and the
                 trainer stops the horse and keeps it in that
                 location for five minutes. The horse is
                 soothed and fed.

STEP 19:   The horse is walked over to the gun and the
                trainer stops the horse and keeps it in that
                location for ten minutes. The horse is
                soothed and fed.

STEP 20:   The horse is walked over to the gun and the
                trainer picks up the gun and holds it for 15
                seconds. The horse is soothed and fed.

STEP 21:   The horse is walked over to the gun and the
                trainer picks up the gun and holds it for 30
                seconds. The horse is soothed and fed.

STEP 22:   The horse is walked over to the gun and the
                trainer picks up the gun and holds it for one
                minute. The horse is soothed and fed.

STEP 23:   The horse is walked over to the gun and the
                trainer picks up the gun and holds it for five
                minutes. The horse is soothed and fed.

STEP 24:   The trainer picks up the gun and mounts the
                horse. The horse is soothed and fed.

STEP 25:   The trainer picks up the gun, mounts and
                rides the horse. The animal is soothed and
                fed.

   The horse is now desensitized to the hunter and to the
gun. Now the animal must be desensitized to the sound of
the gun firing. This may be accomplished in a number of
ways. The most conservative approach is to record the sound
of the gun firing. Then the recording can be paired with the

counterconditioning stimuli (soothing and feeding), and the intensity of the aversive stimulus (gunfire) may be manipulated by increasing the volume of the recording of the gun firing. When the animal reaches a point at which it can tolerate the tape being played at full volume, it may be introduced to the hunter firing the gun. The gun should initially be fired from a considerable distance, so as to minimize the chances of scaring the horse. Then, slowly but surely, the gun can be fired closer to the horse. If this procedure is carefully followed, the horse's anxiety should be eliminated.

Treating Learned Helplessness

Earlier in the chapter we discussed depression and Martin Seligman's concept of learned helplessness. This type of condition is the result of the random administration of punishment and the feeling the animal has that it has no control over its environment. The horse will become very lethargic and will not initiate any type of response behavior. Owners of horses suffering from this condition often become frustrated and punish them. This is the worst possible thing that the horse owner could do. Never punish an animal that is showing symptoms of depression. The cure consists of forced activity and positive reinforcement.

Seligman believes that the only way to deal with this problem is to force the animal to respond. The trainer must physically force the animal to respond and then copiously reinforce it for so doing. The object of this procedure is to actually demonstrate to the horse that it does have control over the consequences of its own behavior.

SUMMARY

We have seen that undesirable behaviors develop under a number of conditions. First, an animal may learn to become anxious in the presence of certain stimuli because those stimuli have been previously associated with an aversive event. This is called a conditioned emotional response, and it interferes with the performance of many healthy behaviors. Second, states of conflict may develop when an animal finds itself in a situation in which it wants to emit two incompatible behaviors at the same time. These states of conflict lead the animal to experience anxiety. Third, repeated trauma or punishment can make an animal very fearful and neurotic. Fourth, if an animal has no control over the consequences of its behavior it will become anxious, listless and depressed.

The procedures described for alleviating an animal's anxiety, depression or undesirable behaviors will usually be effective if they are used properly. They *do* require much time and patience and, unfortunately, if the horse is in an extremely bad state it may not be possible to achieve complete improvement. Usually, if the horse owner is patient, significant improvement can be achieved. As we have emphasized earlier, however, it is always easier to prevent these undesirable emotional states from arising than it is to change them once they have been integrated into the animal's behavioral repertoire. An ounce of prevention is worth a pound of cure!

Bibliography

Azrin, N.H. Some effects of two intermittent schedules of immediate and non-immediate punishment. *Journal of Psychology*, 1956, *42*, 8–21.

———, Holz, W.C., and Hake, D.F. Fixed-ratio punishment. *Journal of the Experimental Analysis of Behavior*, 1963, *6*, 141–148.

Beach, F.A. Evolutionary changes in the psychological control of mating behavior in mammals. *Psychological Review*, 1947, *54*, 297–315.

———, Coital behavior in dogs. III. Effects of early isolation of mating in males. *Behavior*, 1968, *30*, 218–238.

Bokonyi, S. Angaban zur Kenntis der eisenzeit lichen Pferde in Mittleund Osteurop. *Acta Arch. Hungary*, 1964, *12*, 227–239.

———. *History of domestic mammals in central and eastern Europe*. Budapest: Akademiai Kiado, 1974.

Bourliere, F. *The natural history of mammals* (3rd ed.). Toronto: Knopf, 1964.

Carlton, P.L. Brain acetycholine and inhibition. In J. Tapp (Ed.), *Reinforcement and Behavior*. New York: Academic Press, 1969.

Carter, G.S. *Animal evolution*. London: Sidgewick & Jackson, Limited, 1960.

Church, R.M. The varied effects of punishment of behavior. *Psychological Review*, 1963, *70*, 369–402.

Cockrum, E., and Lendell, M. *Introduction to mammalogy*. New York: The Ronald Press Company, 1962.

Daumas, G.E. *The horses of the Sahara.* Austin: University of Texas Press, 1968.

Davis, D.E., and Golley, F.B. *Principles in mammalogy.* New York: Reinhold, 1963.

Desmond, A.J. *The hot-blooded dinosaurs.* New York: The Dial Press, 1976.

Dodson, E.O., and Dodson, P. *Evolution: Process and Product.* New York: Nostrand, 1976.

Eaton, T.H. *Evolution.* New York: Norton, 1970.

Fox, M.W. *Understanding your cat.* New York: Coward, McCann, & Geoghegan, 1974.

Freud, S. Three essays on the theory. In *The standard edition of the complete psychological works of Sigmund Freud.* London: Hogaarth, 1953, Vol. 7, 125–248. (Originally published in 1905.)

Gordon, A., and Bacon, M. Increased efficacy of flooding (response prevention) in rats through positive intracranial stimulation. *Journal of Comparative and Physiological Psychology*, 1971, *75*, 68–72.

Grant, U. *The origin of adaptions.* New York: Columbia University Press, 1967.

Hall, C.S. Temperament: A survey of animal studies. *Psychological Bulletin*, 1941, *38*, 909–943.

Harlow, H.F. Development of affection in primates. In E.L. Bliss (Ed.), *Roots of behavior.* New York: Harper Press, 1962a.

———. The heterosexual affectional system in monkeys. *American Psychologist*, 1962b, *12*.

Hebb, D.O. Spontaneous neuroses in chimpanzees: Theoretical relations with clinical and experimental phenomena. *Psychosomatic Medicine*, 1947, *9*, 3–16.

Hunsicker, J., Nelson, T., and Reid, L.D. *Two kinds of intracranial stimulation as counterconditions of persisting avoidance in rats.* Paper read at the Psychonomic Society, St. Louis, 1972.

Karsh, E. Effects of number of rewarded trials and intensity of punishment on running speed. *Journal of Comparative and Physiological Psychology*, 1962, *55*, 44–51.

Kuo, Z.Y. *The dyanmics of behavior development: An epigenetic view.* New York: Random House, 1967.

Kurstin, I.T. Pavlov's concept of experimental neurosis and abnormal behavior in animals. In M.W. Fox (Ed)., *Abnormal behavior in animals.* Philadelphia: W. B. Saunders, 1968.

Levine, S. Maternal and environmental influences on the adrenocortical response to stress in weanling rats. *Science*, 1967, *156*, 258–260.

————. Infantile experience and consummatory behavior in adulthood. In V.H. Denzenburg (Ed.), *The development of behavior.* Stamford: Sinaver Associates, 1972.

Lorenz, K. *Studies in animal and human behavior. Vol. 1*, trans. R. Martin. Cambridge: Harvard University Press, 1970.

Masserman, J.H. *Behavior and neurosis.* Chicago: University of Chicago Press, 1943.

Miller, N.E. *Neal Miller: Selected papers.* New York: Aldine, Atherton, 1971.

Morris, D. *The mammals.* New York: Harper & Row, 1965.

Murphee, O.D. Inheritance of human aversion and inactivity in two strains of the pointer dog. *Biological Psychiatry*, 1973, *7*, 23–29.

————, and Dykman, R.A. Litter patterns in the offspring of nervous and stable dogs: I. Behavioral tests. *Journal of Nervous and Mental Disease*, 1954, *141*, 321–332.

————, and Newton, J.E. Schizokinesis fragmentation of performance in two strains of pointer dogs. *Conditional Reflex*, 1971, *6*, 91–100.

————, and Dykman, R.A., and Peters, J.E. Genetically determined abnormal behavior in dogs: Results of behavioral tests. *Conditional Reflex*, 1967, *2*, 194.

Pavlov, I.P. *Conditioned reflexes*, trans. G.V. Anrep. London: Oxford University Press, 1927.

Piaget, J. *The development of thought. Equilibrium of cognitive structures*. New York: Viking Press, 1975.

Raymond, P.E. *Prehistoric life*. Cambridge: Harvard University Press, 1967.

Reid, L., Hunsicker, J., Sautter, F., and Miller, H. *Efficient deconditioning of avoidance II*. Presented at the Psychonomic Society Meeting, St. Louis, 1972.

Rower, A.S. *Vertebrate paleontology*. Chicago: The University of Chicago Press, 1966.

————. *Notes and comments on vertebrate paleontology*. Chicago: The University of Chicago Press, 1968.

Salthe, S.N. *Evolutionary biology*. New York: Holt, Rinehart, & Winston, 1972.

Sanson, A. Nouvelle determinations des especes chevalines de genre Equus. *Comp. Rend de l'Acad. d. Scil* Paris, 1869, 69.

Savage, J.M. *Evolution* (3rd ed.). New York: Holt, Rinehart, & Winson, 1977.

Scott, J.P., and Fuller, J.C. *Genetics and the social behavior of the dog*. Chicago: University of Chicago Press, 1965.

Searle, L.V. The organization of hereditary maze-brightness and maze dullness. *Genetic Psychology Monograph, 39*, 279–325, 1949.

Sears, R.R., Maccoby, E.E., and Levin, H. *Patterns of child rearing*. Evanston: Row, Peterson, 1957.

Seitz, P.F. Infantile experience and adult behavior in animal subjects: II. Age of separation from the mother and behavior in the cat. *Psychosomatic Medicine*, 1959, *21*, 353–378.

Seligman, M.E. Chronic fear produced by unpredictable shock. *Journal of Comparative and Physiological Psychology*, 1968, *66*, 402–411.

————. *Helplessness: On depression, development, and death.* San Francisco: W. H. Freeman and Company, 1975.

Simpson, G.G. *Horses.* New York: Doubleday, 1951 (1961).

Skinner, B.F. *The behavior of organisms.* New York: Appleton Century, 1938.

Solomon, R.L. Punishment. *American Psychologist,* 1964, *19,* 239–252.

————, and Wynne, L.C. Traumatic avoidance learning: The principles of anxiety conservation and partial irreversibility. *Psychological Review,* 1954, *61,* 353–385.

————, Turner, L.H., and Lessac, M.S. Some effects of delay of punishment on resistance to temptation in dogs. *Journal of Personality and Social Psychology,* 1968, *8,* 233–238.

Stanley, W.C., and Elliot, O. Differential human handling as reinforcing events and as treatments influencing later social behavior in Basenji puppies. *Psychological Reports,* 1962, *10,* 775–788.

Summerhays, R.S. *Encyclopedia for horsemen.* London: Frederick Warne and Company, Ltd. 1966.

Vaura, R. *Such is the real nature of horses.* New York: William Morrow and Company, Inc., 1979.

Walker, E.P. *Mammals of the world.* Baltimore: The Johns Hopkins Press, 1968.

Winchester, A.M. *Heredity evolution and humankind.* New York: West, 1976.

Wolpe, J. Experimental neurosis as a learned behavior. *British Journal of Psychology,* 1952, *43,* 243–268.

————. *Psychotherapy by reciprocal inhibition.* Stanford, California: Stanford University Press, 1958.

————. The conditioning and deconditioning of neurotic anxiety. In C.D. Spielburger (Ed.), *Anxiety and behavior.* New York: Academic Press, 1966.

Woolpy, J.H., and Ginsburg, B.E. Wolf socialization: A study of temperament in a wild social species. *American Zoologist*, 1967, *7*, 357–363.

Index

Schedules of reinforcement,
100–102
Schedule stretching, 101–102
Secondary reinforcers, 95
Shaping, 97–100
Shetland Pony, 55
Shire, 59
Sign stimuli, 13
Skewbald, 50
Socialization process, 4–5
Species, 33–38
Species specific, 13
Standardbred, 48–49
Stimuli, 93–97
Stimulus discrimination,
99–100
Stimulus generalization, 100
Stimulus hierarchy, 130–137
Suffolk, 60
Symmedtrodonta, 26
Systematic desensitization,
130–137

Tapiridae, 28
Tarpon, 6, 34, 35
Tennessee Walking Horse, 53

Theoretical basis of
psychology, 14–16
Therasipid, 25
Thoroughbred, 16, 47
Titantotheres, 28–29
Training, 8, 91–137
need for, 8
removal of fears, 109–137
Triassic mammals, 25
Tricondonta, 26

Ungulates, 25
Unlearned reinforcers, 94

Variable schedules, 101–102
Variables in behavior, 9–10

Warm blooded animals, 25
Welsh Mountain Pony,
55–56
Western Asian wild horse, 35
Wild ass, 38
Wild horses, 35
Working horses, 2

Zebras, 36–38